handy homework helper

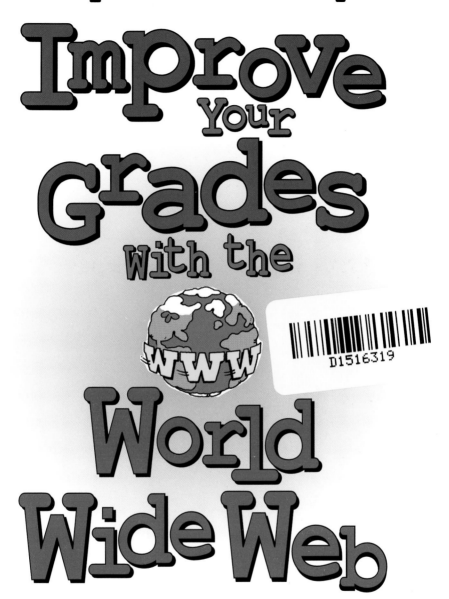

Improve Your Grades with the World Wide Web

Karen Cangero, M.S.

Consultant:
Marc Alan Rosner

Publications International, Ltd.

Karen Cangero has a masters degree in education and writes often about the Internet, education, and children. She contributes regularly to the KidsHealth Web site (http://www.KidsHealth.org/), *Web Guide* magazine, and other publications. The Internet is Ms. Cangero's lifeline to the rest of the world from her farmhouse in upstate New York.

Marc Alan Rosner is an education technology support specialist in New York, New York, and an educational consultant to *Scientific American* magazine. His published books include *Teaching Science with the Internet, Teaching Mathematics with the Internet,* and *Science Fair Success Using the Internet.* Mr. Rosner has been awarded fellowships for excellence in education by The Joseph Klingenstein Institute, The New York Times Foundation, and the Charles Edison Fund.

Illustrators: Dave Garbot, Chris Reed

Louis Weber, C.E.O.
Publications International, Ltd.
7373 North Cicero Avenue
Lincolnwood, Illinois 60646

Manufactured in China.

8 7 6 5 4 3 2 1

ISBN: 0-7853-3489-0

Contents

A Message to Parents

In the last few years, we have seen the World Wide Web rapidly develop into an important educational tool. And with each passing year, the number of school districts throughout the country that are introducing or expanding their educational technology facilities, curriculum, and overall expectations grows.

However, letting your child loose on the "Information Superhighway" can be frightening. Technology is vastly different today than it was just ten years ago, not to mention when you were in school. Today's kids will need to be able to utilize the online world in order to compete in school—and eventually the job market—of the twenty-first century.

The goal of this book is to help kids use the World Wide Web to improve their grades in school. Searching for information is the key to using the Web successfully. A large portion of *Handy Homework Helper: Improve Your Grades With the World Wide Web* is devoted to explaining and demonstrating how to perform various types of searches. We'll discuss using the Web to help with homework, test-taking, writing reports, and other projects. This book puts these important scholastic features into the overall context of becoming the best student possible. And this includes important safety tips and how to use the Web as a brainstorming tool for activities kids get involved in when they step away from the computer.

The Web is an amazing place, where children can see images from half a world away—or even another planet—and have access to limitless educational materials. However, not everything that exists on the Web is appropriate for children. Close parental supervision and guidance are essential in making your children's online journeys safe, educational, and fun. These steps can help keep your children away from inappropriate sites.

- Discuss with your children what sorts of Web sites they may visit.

- Discuss what to do if they accidentally stumble upon an inappropriate site.

- Encourage them to come to you with questions if material puzzles or disturbs them.

- Be sure they come to you for permission and assistance before spending money on the Internet.

- Put the computer in a "public" room. Keeping the computer in the family room, living room, or den makes online exploration a group activity.

- Use software and online services that filter inappropriate material.

- Discuss when to—and when not to—use e-mail and chat rooms.

Both Windows 95 and 98 include options to screen Web sites based on the renowned Recreational Software Advisory Council rating service for the Internet (RSACi) system. RSACi is the World Wide Web's most prevalent ratings system. It lets you control access to content on the Web. Not every site out there is rated, but many are. Most online service providers also let you restrict your child's access to the Web, chat rooms, and other online features. There are a number of software packages available that try to keep kids safer on the Web. Some popular software packages include CyberSitter, Net Nanny, and SurfWatch. For more information on kids' safety and the World Wide Web visit http://www.zen.org/~brendan/kids-safe.html.

Partners in Your Child's Education

Parents play an important role in their children's scholastic success. Research has proven that what families do together is much more important to student success than whether people are rich or poor or whether or not parents have finished high school. This applies throughout your kids' education—from elementary through high school.

To focus more attention on this important subject, the United States Congress recently added a seventh point to their list of six National Education Goals, which states: "Every school will promote partnerships that will increase parental involvement and participation in promoting the social, emotional, and academic growth of children."

Homework is an opportunity for students to expand learning outside of the classroom and for parents to get involved in their children's education. A parent's interest can spark enthusiasm in a child and help teach them the most important lesson of all—that learning can be fun and is well worth the effort. Homework can also bring parents and educators closer together. Parents who supervise homework and monitor their children's assignments learn about their children's education and school.

Teachers assign homework for many reasons. Homework can help children:

- Review and practice what they've learned.

- Get ready for the next day's class.

- Learn to use resources, such as libraries, online materials, reference materials, and encyclopedias.

- Explore subjects more fully than time permits in the classroom.

Homework can also help children develop good habits and attitudes. It can:

- Teach children to work independently.

- Encourage self-discipline and responsibility.

- Provide young students with their first chance to manage time and meet deadlines.

- Encourage a love of learning.

Show You Think Education and Homework Are Important

The U.S. Department of Education has some specific guidelines for helping your children with their homework. Children need to know that their parents and adults close to them think homework is important. If they know that their parents care, children have a good reason to always try to complete assignments and turn them in on time. There is a lot that you can do as parents to show that you value education and homework.

- Set a regular study time and place.

- Remove distractions from the study area.

- Provide study supplies and, if possible, any available resource materials.

- Set a good example by spending your time reading and writing and limiting your television time.

- Show interest by talking about school and related projects and by taking family trips to the library and other learning locations.

Monitor Assignments

Children are more likely to complete assignments successfully when parents monitor homework. How closely you need to monitor depends upon the age of your child, how independent they are, and how well they do in school. Whatever the age of your child, if assignments are not being satisfactorily completed, more supervision is needed. Be sure to:

- Ask about the teacher's homework policy at the beginning of the school year.

- Be available to provide assistance and to answer questions during homework time.

- Read over completed assignments and provide constructive criticism.

In addition to helping with homework, there are other ways that parents can assist in their children's learning process.

- Encourage children to spend more leisure time reading than watching television.

- Talk with your children in order to communicate positive behavior and character traits.

- Keep in touch with the school and other organizations your children are associated with.

- Encourage your children's efforts to achieve.

Working with your children as they learn more about education and the world can be some of the most rewarding times of development. And learning about the Web is an activity that will continue for years. Good luck and remember to make learning fun!

What is the World Wide Web?

Fasten your seat belts. Keep your arms inside the vehicle. We are currently speeding up the ramp to the "Information Superhighway." Accessing information. Logging on. Successful. Welcome to the wonderful world of the World Wide Web!

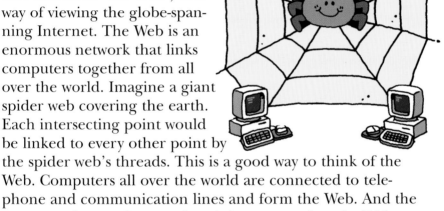

The World Wide Web (otherwise known as "the Web") is a way of viewing the globe-spanning Internet. The Web is an enormous network that links computers together from all over the world. Imagine a giant spider web covering the earth. Each intersecting point would be linked to every other point by the spider web's threads. This is a good way to think of the Web. Computers all over the world are connected to telephone and communication lines and form the Web. And the computer in your home, when it is connected to the Web, can then communicate with any other computer connected to the World Wide Web.

Many people think that the Web and the Internet are the same thing. They're not.

The Internet is a worldwide collection of computer networks that allows people to find and use information and communicate. It was started in the 1960s by the U.S. Department of Defense. Soon researchers and university professors began to use it, too. It made communicating and getting information much easier.

The World Wide Web is a way of viewing the Internet. The Web mostly uses pictures to communicate. However, words are also everywhere as well as videos, animations, and sounds. All of these parts of the Web work together to make it a truly multimedia experience!

What makes the World Wide Web truly a "Web," separating it from the rest of the Internet, are hyperlinks (also just called "links"). A link can be a word, a picture, or an icon (like the pictures you click on your computer desktop)—or even a group of words or part of a picture. Links refer to other pages—either within that same Web site or anywhere else on the Web. Clicking on a link brings up its corresponding page. Thanks to hyperlinks, you can easily surf from page to page and site to site—just by clicking your mouse!

Important Web Words

First, let's define some important words that we will be using (if any other words that come up in this book are confusing, check their definitions in the Glossary, on pages 122–125).

Web Site and Web Page. The Web is made up of an ever-growing number of Web pages. A Web page is different from a page in a book. Web pages can hold many pages of information. A Web site can have one or a lot of pages that share one Web address. If this confuses you, think of a household. A family with many people sharing one house is a household. But so is one person living alone. It's the same with Web sites—you'll find sites that have only one page and sites that have a lot of pages.

Need an ISP?

If you don't have an Internet service provider yet, go to the library with your parents and use a public computer there (or use a friend's computer) to check out a list of local ISPs at: http://www.thelist.com. If a computer that is hooked up to the Internet is not available, check your local yellow pages.

Home Page. A site's home page is the page that shows up on your computer screen when you first arrive at the site. It's like looking at the cover of a book. Usually, a home page will tell you a bit about the site and have links that you can follow. These links may lead you to other pages in that site or to other sites on the Web.

Web Server. Web pages and sites are stored on computers called Web servers. These servers store information and send requested pages to browsers. The Web is actually a worldwide network of Web servers.

Internet Service Provider (ISP). Internet service providers, sometimes called online services, are the gatekeepers of the Internet. Your ISP provides you with the software and the telephone connection you need to get online. To get onto the Internet, a computer must call up its ISP. Then, the ISP connects the computer to the Internet and the Web. Many people use their online service—such as America Online or Microsoft Network—as their ISP. Others use a local ISP.

URL. Uniform Resource Locator. That's a fancy way of saying Web address. Every Web page has its own address on the Internet. No other page has the same URL. At first, URLs may look like a jumble of letters, numbers, periods, and slashes, but there is a system to how they work. In this book, some listed URLs have hyphens in them when they run from one line to the next. These hyphens, when used at the end of a line, are not part of the address. They are just like hyphens in a word that runs from one line to the next. See page 90 for an example of this use of hyphens (in the URL for Ask an Expert). See pages 25–27 for more information on Web addresses.

Browser. A browser is software that lets computers display Web sites and pages, including any text, sound clips, pictures, videos, or animation on a Web page. Browsers also let you use hyperlinks. Most people use Netscape Navigator or Microsoft Internet Explorer as their browser (both of these browsers are free). A complete discussion of browsers is on pages 21–25.

Bookmark. A bookmark is a saved link. Bookmarks are called Favorites in Internet Explorer. They are usually stored in a folder in the browser. These links make returning to favorite sites easy. Simply click on the bookmark. Your browser will take you to the saved page. That way, you don't have to locate and retype the URL each time you visit a favorite Web page.

Web Uses

People who use the Web have access to research materials, news, shopping, entertainment, tons of information, and all kinds of other stuff. We will explore the Web's educational resources in later chapters. Here are some other ways people use the Web.

E-mail. Electronic mail (e-mail) is the most popular part of the Internet. E-mail is like regular mail, but it lets you send and receive "letters" with your computer. You can usually get free e-mail software from your ISP or browser company. In addition to sending a simple e-mail message, you can include attachments. An attachment can be a picture, video or sound clip, or another letter. Any file on your hard drive can be attached to e-mail. However, not all e-mail programs are set up to send and receive some attachments (such as sounds, videos, or pictures).

Warning!

Viruses can be attached to e-mail messages. If you aren't sure that an e-mail file attachment is safe, *do not download it*! Downloading a virus can cause a lot of trouble for your computer (it can even erase your hard drive!). However, just opening and reading an e-mail message cannot activate a virus or harm your computer.

Usenet Newsgroups. Newsgroups are huge discussion groups involving people from all over the world. These are basically electronic bulletin boards where people post messages for each other. Each board focuses on a particular topic. The messages can be read by anyone visiting the bulletin board and anyone can post a message.

Because newsgroups are not managed by anyone, you need to be careful when using them. The bulletin boards often become clogged with bogus get-rich-quick schemes and offensive material.

Newsgroups are organized by category (called hierarchies)—each dedicated to a specific topic.

Some interesting hierarchies are:

- Newusers. A good starting point.
- K12. Topics for teachers and students from kindergarten through 12th grade.
- Schl. More educational newsgroups.
- News. Discussions on news and current events.
- SCI. Science.
- Soc. Society and cultures.

Chat. "Let your fingers do the talking!" Of course, kids' computers do the talking, not their mouths. Messages are typed back and forth. That's what chatting is all about. Chatting is a great way to meet different people. Chatting is done in "chat rooms." Everyone in the chat room can read and respond to the message. Many Web sites provide chat rooms for kids on a variety of topics.

Web safety is a big issue today. Several companies provide kids-only chat rooms that are closely monitored. Still, kids shouldn't log into a new chat room without their parents'

Kids Only!

Here are some kid-friendly chat rooms:
- **Freezone** (http://chat.freezone.com) Fully monitored chat area for kids only. Chat topics include: All-Grrls Chat, All-Guyz Chat, Music and Movies Chat, and Homework Help Chat.
- **Headbone Zone Chat for Kids** (http://ykd.headbone.com/hbzchat) Fully monitored kids-only chat. Chat rooms, e-mail, games, and activities.
- **Kidlink** (http://www.kidlink.org) Kids cross cultural boundaries here.

permission. Be sure to read the Web safety rules (see pages 43–45) before going into a chat room.

Information Gathering. The Web can be considered the biggest reference library in the world. Much of this book discusses research on the Web. Besides research, you can use the Web to get news and information. Millions of people log on the Web daily to check the news, weather, and sports scores. These sites will keep you up to the minute (and give you something to talk about during current events at school!):

- **The Associated Press** (http://www.ap.org). The world's oldest and largest news organization. Check out "The Wire" for the latest headlines.

- **Reuters News Room** (http://www.reuters.com/news). News organization providing headlines and in-depth reports. Covers top stories, business news, sports, and more.

- **Children's Express** (http://www.ce.org). Kids age 8–18 write this monthly news service.

- **Intellicast** (http://www.intellicast.com). Outstanding weather site. Check out your forecast and take a look at interactive maps, almanac facts, and more.

- **Sports Network** (http://www.sportsnetwork.com).
  Check out scores, stats, and stories.

Shopping. Web shopping has become a multi-billion dollar industry. You can find anything on the Web. Virtual stores are never closed. Some of these stores only exist on the Web—such as Amazon.com. Always be sure to ask your parents for permission before purchasing anything on the Web.

Entertainment. The Web has more information than you could read in a lifetime. Thankfully, it has outlets for fun too. Want to try some new computer games? Need to know which new movies are good? Want to find out the latest gossip on the hippest new bands or TV shows? The Web has it all—plus more! Dig into online games, contests, jokes, screensavers, movies, TV, music, and more.

There's a lot of free stuff on the Web too. If you know how to get it, it's yours! In Chapter 7 (see page 95), we'll discuss finding and downloading files to your computer. Downloading means copying a file from another computer. Many sites gather files—such as photos, maps, and games—for downloading.

An Educational Web?

Now we know that the Web is part of a huge, linked computer network. You can use it to locate lots of information, to communicate, even to shop. But, can using the Web really improve grades? Yes! By using the Web wisely, students can:

- Get homework help. Online reference materials—such as encyclopedias and dictionaries—provide access to a multitude of information.

- Communicate with other students, educators, and experts.

- Research topics for papers and other projects. Search engines and directories find information on any subject.

- Improve problem-solving skills. Good searches require thought and analysis.

- Discover places around the world and learn about other cultures.

- Gain technology skills. Obtain hands-on experience with skills needed in education and the workplace.

- Have fun! The Web offers lots of interactive chances for combining learning and entertainment.

It's important to remember that the Web doesn't have a boss or a principal. Everyone who posts information on the Web helps build it. Of course, some sources are more reliable than others. When you're gathering research for a report or other project, make sure you think about your sources. Which is a more reliable reference for a report on butterflies: an encyclopedia or your neighbor's little brother Bobby? Go with the encyclopedia. It's possible that Bobby is a well-known butterfly expert, but the information in an encyclopedia is double- and even tripled-checked for correctness; butterfly-lovin' Bobby isn't.

The Web works the same way. While some butterfly buffs may have home pages devoted to butterflies, you can't be sure that they're accurate. It is always better to use established reference materials. Using good reference sources is covered in-depth on pages 40–43.

When to Use the Web

The Web is an important information source. But remember that it is just one part of your study routine. Traditional study and research skills are still very important. Search the Web for information. But also check your school and local libraries for resources. And of course your school textbooks and class handouts are other places to find information. Use the Web as an extra library to find facts. It isn't meant to replace the encyclopedia at the library or the notes you take in class.

One cool part of the Web is its speed. The Web is a great place to look for information if you don't have much time for research. Doing a search takes time, but the Web is never closed. Sundays, evenings, holidays— you can always browse the Web.

Of course, the Web isn't just for schoolwork. It's a place to find games, make friends, read about a hobby or interest, and more. However, just like TV time, Web time should be limited too. Be sure to plan time for other activities besides surfing the Web. Playing outside, reading a book, talking with your friends, doing your chores and homework, and spending time with your family are all important too.

How to Get to the Web

Now that we have most of the Web basics under out belts, let's get surfing! Your parents should have already done the following steps in order to connect to the Internet. (One exception is Web TV; see pages 20–21.) You need:

1. A computer. A Macintosh or PC (personal computer) with at least 16 MB of RAM.

2. A modem. Modems let computers talk to each other. They connect to telephone lines. There are both internal and external modems. Popular modems today are 28.8 kbps, 33.6 kbps, and 56.6 kbps. "Kbps" stands for kilobits-per-second. This is the speed of the modem (like miles-per-hour in the car). These speeds tell how fast the computer can get information from other computers. Some computers still have 14.4 kbps modems, but the Web is getting too big and fast for these to work very well.

3. An Internet service provider. See page 13 for more information on ISPs.

4. A browser. See pages 21–25 for more on browsers.

Connecting to the Web is pretty painless.

- First, turn on the computer.

- Once the computer has warmed up, select the ISP or browser icon (usually by double clicking on it).

- Select connect. (Not always necessary, depending on software.)

- Enter your username and password. (All ISPs require these, although sometimes they are stored in the computer and don't need to be entered each time. If that is the case, the connection will be automatic.)

If this has been done correctly, two things should happen:

- The modem makes beeps, dings, and static noises as your computer connects with the ISP's computer.

- The browser's home page will then be displayed.

Web TV

Web TV gives you access to the World Wide Web through your television. You don't even have to have a computer! If you have a TV and a telephone, you can use Web TV. In most cases, Web TV works just like a computer for browsing the

Web. You can even use a printer to print out your local TV listings. Web TV connects you to the Internet and provides you with tools that make surfing the Net easy and enjoyable. Just hit the GOTO button, type in the address of the site you want to visit, and you're on your way.

The directions and examples used in this book will usually describe Web browsing with regular computers. If you're using Web TV you can easily follow the same steps. Just remember to use your handy GOTO button to get you wherever you want to go.

Browsers are your window to the Web.

The address location box is your ticket to visiting Web sites.

The Browser Window

Netscape Navigator (just Netscape for short) and Microsoft Internet Explorer (Explorer) are the most popular Web browsers. They both do very similar things, but they also have some differences.

Menu Bar. Just like all computer programs, your browser will have a menu bar. Every available function is on the menu bar. Many of the menu functions will be familiar to you from other programs. For example, using the menu bar, you can: open files; cut, copy, and paste; and get help.

Toolbar. The toolbar is located just below the menu bar. It is also called a button bar. Toolbar buttons help you navigate around Web pages.

Some buttons are found on the toolbar in both Netscape Navigator and Internet Explorer:

Back. Your browser keeps track of where you've been on the Web. It remembers every page you visit. This feature is help-

Get Current! Update!

Want to get the latest copy of Netscape Navigator or Microsoft Internet Explorer? Download them from the Web! For Navigator, go to http://www.netscape.com/download; for Explorer go to http://www.microsoft.com/msdownload. Make sure you have your parents help you if you want to download the most recent version of one of these free browsers.

ful because after a few minutes of following links you can be far away from where you started. Clicking the Back button on the toolbar takes you, with each click, back page by page to where you started.

Forward. If you go back too far, click Forward. This button moves you up one page at a time in your Web history. This only works if you have used your Back or Home buttons to revisit previous pages.

Home. Displays your home page. This is the page that you tell your browser to show when you log on. By default (that means automatically), the home page is usually your browser's home page. Other choices you might consider are a search engine or other favorite Web site. This is usually set up in the Preferences (or Options) section of your browser.

Reload/Refresh. Redisplays the current page. Your browser checks the current page against the one in your history. If there are changes, the new page is loaded. If not, the same page is loaded again. This function is useful when visiting any World Wide Web site that updates information often, such as http://www.espn.com for sports scores.

Stop. Stops the current transmission. As soon as you begin loading a page, the Stop button becomes active. Use the Stop button when you have accidentally asked for the wrong page or the page that you have requested hasn't loaded after a long wait (when this happens, it usually means that there is a problem with that page).

Print. Lets you print the current window. Make sure that the window you want to print is the one that you are currently on.

Other buttons on Netscape's toolbar let you:

- **Open** a Web page by typing its URL.
- **Find** a word or phrase in the current page.

Other buttons on Explorer's toolbar let you:

- **Search** for information on the Web.
- Flip through Microsoft's pre-selected **Channels.**
- Collect and visit your personal Web **Favorites.**
- Read and write **Mail.**

Address Location Box. Below the toolbar, you will find the address location box. This feature serves two functions.

1. It displays the address of the page your browser is currently showing or downloading.

2. It instructs the browser to retrieve any address you type into the box. (Hit Enter on your keyboard after typing the desired address to begin loading the new page.)

Explorer has a nice feature called the AutoComplete. As you begin typing a URL in the address box, it automatically searches your history. If it finds a match, Explorer suggests the site. That way, you can get to a Web site after only typing a few letters in the address location box.

Logo Box. To the right of the toolbar or the address locator box you will find the logo box. This box contains the logo for the browser you use. Netscape's logo box is an "N" on a shoot-

Here's a Tip

If a download seems endless, check your logo box. If it stays animated for a long time, you may want to click the Stop or Reload/Refresh buttons on your toolbar. This usually means that something is wrong with the requested page (like it is under construction or just not working at the moment).

ing stars background. Explorer's logo box features Microsoft's "flying window" that rotates into a globe. Besides advertising the browser's company, the logo box is a status gauge. When the logo is animated (the picture is moving), it means that a transfer is in progress.

Scroll bars. These may appear on the right side and/or bottom of your browser window. Depending on the size of the window that you are viewing, you may need to scroll to see the entire page. The scroll bars work just like the ones you have in almost all other programs. Your browser window can sometimes be adjusted to make the page fit on the screen by clicking the boxes at the corners of your screen.

Status bar. The status bar is usually along the bottom of your browser screen and provides important information about what your browser is doing. As a page is downloading, the status bar sometimes displays the name of the page it is retrieving. It keeps you informed of the browser's progress as it contacts, retrieves, and loads a page. When downloading a file, the status bar tells you how many items are waiting to download or the percentage of the file left to download. When you position your cursor over a link, the status bar displays the URL of that link's Web page.

World Wide Web Addresses

Just like the houses in your town, every Web site has an address. These are also known as URLs. There is a system (called a protocol) to naming Web sites. Knowing this protocol's rules can help you understand and remember a Web site's address.

Nearly all URLs begin with "http://." This tells your computer that the address points to a hypertext document—a Web page. "Http" actually stands for "hypertext transfer protocol."

Next, in most Web page addresses, comes "www." This lets you know that the site is on the World Wide Web.

The next part of the URL is usually the name of the site's organization. This portion of the URL may be the organization's name spelled out, an abbreviation of the name, or a different name altogether. This part of the address is called the domain. For example, the domain name for the Public Broadcasting System's Web site is "pbs." Think of the domain name as the name of the city in your street address.

Finally, the last part of the URL (or the "suffix") provides information about the type of organization maintaining the site. Common suffixes are:

- .com. This is for companies and other commercial Web sites.

- .edu. For educational facilities, such as colleges, school districts, and some research facilities.

- .org. For nonprofit organizations.

- .gov. For government organizations.

- .mil. For military branches and facilities.

By knowing this system, you can sometimes guess a Web site's address. For example, if you were trying to find the Yale University home page, you might try typing "http://www.yale.edu" into your address location box. (And you would be correct!)

Sometimes slashes separate parts of longer Web addresses. Each directory, subdirectory, and file name follow a slash. Your browser knows that a slash means that the address is getting more specific.

For example, the American Library Association (ALA) site has a section called KidsConnect. At KidsConnect, you can get homework help from a real librarian. Members of the

ALA check the site's e-mail regularly and respond to students' questions. It is possible that you would be able to follow the links to this great homework help section of the ALA Web site from the sites's home page. However, if you know the full address to get to the KidsConnect section, you can go there right away!

The first part of the address directs you to the American Library Association's Web site (http://www.ala.org). But that's not the entire address for KidsConnect yet!

The KidsConnect pages are in the "ICONN" directory at the American Library Association's site. You need to add "ICONN" to the address: "http://www.ala.org/ICONN."

Next, we need to get to the KidsConnect page. The code for that page is "AskKC.html." Now our complete address for the American Library Association's KidsConnect page is: "http://www.ala.org/ICONN/ AskKC.html." That's quite a mouthful!

Enough Stretching! Let's Surf!

You should be pretty stretched out by now and ready to jump into the ocean of the World Wide Web. With the basics and safety tips under your belt, you will be able to work wonders with the Web. The following chapters will open up a new world of possibility for your school activities, homework assignments, reports, projects, hobbies, and other interests. And, chances are that by the time you are through, you will have learned something new. Maybe you will find new interests along the way. One thing is for sure: You will never look at your computer the same way again. But enough already! Let's start surfing!

Chapter 1
Getting Started

Victoria's third grade class has been learning about computers and the Internet. She has a computer at home. She mostly uses it to write letters, play games, and paint pictures. And she had never been on the Internet or the World Wide Web before. But last week, Victoria's class learned about some of the things that people can do on the Web. Victoria and her class recently visited the library computer room and went online for the first time. Here's what they did.

Each student sat down at a computer and turned on the power. Victoria's teacher, Ms. Moore, said that this is called "booting up." Then Ms. Moore gave the class these instructions.

1. Find the "My Computer" icon in the top left corner of your desktop. Double-click on it.

2. In the My Computer window (which you just opened), find the "Dial-up Networking" icon. Double-click on it.

3. In the Dial-up Networking window, find the "Internet Connection" icon. Double-click on it.

4. In the Internet Connection window, click just once on "Connect" at the bottom of the window.

5. A new kind of window, called a "status" window, will open. The status window, and the status bar in the window, let you know that the computer is busy getting you online.

6. The status bar will disappear once you have been connected to the Internet.

Victoria followed Ms. Moore's instructions carefully. She had a little trouble finding the "Connect" button, but Ms. Moore helped her. Then Victoria watched the status window. First, it said "Dialing." After a minute it said, "Establishing Network Connection." Then the window let Victoria know that the computer was "Verifying User Name and Password." Finally, it said "Logging onto Network." Then it suddenly disappeared! Victoria was online!

Your software may be set up so that your browser automatically opens when an Internet connection is made. If you need some help getting online, ask your parents.

Victoria's class connected to the Internet using their school's Internet service provider (ISP). Now they need to connect to their browser in order to go anywhere on the Web. Remember that a browser is software that brings up Web pages on your computer.

Once a Web connection has been made, double-click on your browser icon. Icons are little pictures that represent the programs on your computer. They are usually displayed somewhere on the screen (called the "desktop"). The position of your icons depends upon your computer and how it is set up.

Get Connected!

The steps for connecting to the Internet may be different for you. It depends on how your computer and software are set up. Some ways you might connect to the Internet are by:
- Double-clicking on your browser icon.
- Double-clicking on your online service icon.
- Double-clicking on your Internet service provider (ISP) icon.

Victoria double-clicked on the Netscape Navigator icon on the left side of her desktop. Then the browser window opened. Ms. Moore explained that the logo box and status bar show that the browser is loading a page. Victoria watched the stars fly in the Netscape logo box. The status bar slowly filled up, from left to right, and counted up to 100 percent as the page loaded. When it is first started, a browser loads its designated home page.

After the browser's home page had loaded, Ms. Moore handed out a list of the week's vocabulary words. But instead of looking up the words in the classroom dictionaries as the students usually would, they were instructed to use an online dictionary. Ms. Moore then explained how to get to the Merriam-Webster online dictionary.

1. Click on the address location box. The address will become highlighted and a blinking cursor will appear.

2. Type "http://www.m-w.com" in the address location box. The old address should disappear as soon as you start typing.

3. Hit "Enter."

Personalize Your Browser

A browser's home page is different than a Web site's home page. You can set your browser to open any Web page you like whenever it is opened. That page is called the browser's home page. By default (that means automatically), it's usually your browser's home page. For example, Netscape Navigator's default home page is Netscape's home page. You can change which page the browser goes to when you start it in the Options menu of your browser. Select General Preferences. . . . The address of the home page can be entered on this screen. Enter any Web address you wish: your favorite search engine, homework help page, games center, and so on.

Look It Up!

The Merriam-Webster site (http://www.m-w.com) is much more than a dictionary. It's a free language center. Just like the regular dictionary, each word is followed by the pronunciation, part of speech, definitions, and some historical information. However, the online M-W dictionary uses the word in a sentence or phrase and gives you more information about the word's history. There are also word games, a thesaurus, detailed descriptions of "cool words," and lots of other useful features. If you really want to get smart, check out the word of the day, every day!

Victoria watched as the Merriam-Webster Web site appeared on her screen. She did it! She's on the Web. She carefully typed her vocabulary words one at a time in the "WWWebster Dictionary" box and searched for their definitions. The site gave her lots of helpful information, including a sentence that used the word.

Next, Ms. Moore showed the class how to save the Merriam-Webster Web site as a "Bookmark." Bookmarks are saved links to your favorite pages. Then, in the future, when you want to return to that site, you can do so with just a simple click. That way you don't have to remember and retype the site's address every time you visit!

To save the Merriam-Webster site as a bookmark, Victoria followed these instructions.

1. Make sure you are on the home page of the Merriam-Webster Web site. If not, use the "Back" button to return to the site's home page.

2. Go to the "Bookmarks" (or "Favorites") menu and pull it down.

3. Select "Add Bookmark."

Working with Bookmarks

Bookmarks make using the Web much easier. Using bookmarks, you can return to favorite or helpful pages again and again with little effort. There are several ways to bookmark a page. The first thing you need to do is to make sure that the page you want to bookmark is the one currently shown on your browser.

To add a bookmark in Netscape Navigator (or "NN" for short):

First, make sure you are on the exact page you want to bookmark.

Pull down the "Bookmarks" menu.

Select "Add Bookmark."

Other ways to add a bookmark are to hold down the "CTRL" (or "Command," known as the "Apple Key" on Macintosh computers) key and then hit the "D" key or to click your right-hand mouse button and select "Add Bookmark."

To add a bookmark in Internet Explorer:

First, make sure you are on the exact page you want to bookmark.

Pull down the "Favorites" menu.

Select "Add to Favorites . . ." or click your right-hand mouse button and select "Add to Favorites. . . ."

When you add a Web page to the Favorites in Internet Explorer (or "IE" for short), you need to decide if you want to "subscribe" to that site. Subscribing means that IE will check those Web sites every so often for new content. You can tell IE to check your subscribed sites for new material daily, weekly, or monthly. Then you can choose either to be notified that there is new content available on one of your subscribed sites or to have the updated content automatically downloaded (see page 95) to your hard drive. This type of subscribing isn't like paying for a regular magazine or newspaper delivery. This doesn't cost anything.

If you choose to have new stuff from your "subscriptions" automatically downloaded to your hard drive, you can then check out your favorite Web sites offline at your leisure. However, subscribing can take up a lot of space on your hard drive. Talk with your parents about this IE option.

If you can't find a bookmark that you are looking for, or your list is too long to read quickly, you can use the "Find" feature. Pull down the Edit menu and select Find. In the window that appears, type the name of the Web site that you're looking for. If you can't remember its exact name, enter a word or two from that site's address that you do know. Your browser will find any links containing those words. Then you can double-click on the right address to load that page.

Organizing Your Bookmarks

Victoria is starting to feel more comfortable on the Web. She's been doing some online stuff for school (such as a report on the weather) and some just for fun. But her list of bookmarks is getting too long. She sometimes has trouble finding a specific site.

Luckily, both NN and IE have features to let Victoria organize her bookmarked links. She can put similar bookmarks in handy folders (such as putting all of her homework help bookmarks together) in order to organize her bookmark list. Then she can give the new folder a name. Here's how she organized her bookmarks for the Web sites she is using to do her report for school.

1. In the Bookmarks menu, Victoria selected "Item" and then "Insert Folder."

2. Then, the "Bookmark Properties" window opened.

3. In the "Name" text box, Victoria typed "Weather Report."

4. In the "Description" text box, Victoria typed "Sites for my report on the weather."

5. Victoria then clicked "OK" to close the Bookmark Properties window.

To move the bookmarks into this folder, Victoria simply clicked and dragged each bookmark onto the folder. When she held the bookmark over the folder, the folder changed color and she let go of her mouse button. Now that bookmark has been placed into a folder!

Victoria repeated the same steps to create other folders for school and fun sites. The next time Victoria opens her bookmarks, instead of a long, confusing list of links, she will see her neat list of folders. Now she'll quickly know where to find any site she is looking for!

Megadirectories and Search Engines

The Web grows constantly—every day, every hour, every minute. It has more information than any library in the world. Anyone can put information on the Web. It's easy and free! This is both good and bad.

The good news is that whatever you are looking for is probably on the Web—somewhere. The bad news is that you're going to have to search through an amazing amount of information to find what you're looking for.

Luckily, some Web services exist just to help you find what you need. Megadirectories help Web users by sorting Web

Bookmark Bonuses

You'll notice that when you pull down the Bookmarks menu that no actual Web addresses are listed. For example, instead of seeing "http://www.weather.com" you'll see "The Weather Channel" listed. These titles describe the book-marked Web page. That way you don't need to remember all of the letters, dots, or slashes in Web addresses. Bookmarks make browsing much easier!

sites into categories (just like Victoria, when she created folders for her list of bookmarks). Then you can search through the categories, and their many levels, to find the sites that you are look-ing for.

Search engines, on the other hand, do the looking for you. You type in words that describe what you're looking for. These words are called keywords. Hit "Start Search" or some similar command, and the search engine quickly looks all over the Web and returns a list of links to sites that match your keywords. Both megadirectories and search engines help you find what you need, but they work very differently. Many search tools today act as both megadirectories and search engines. This lets you perform a search in whatever way is best for you.

Megadirectories

Megadirectories have many levels. The top level is the largest. This level sorts Web sites into some general categories; then come the subcategories, sub-subcategories, and so on. Unfortunately, no one megadirectory can list every Web site out there. Why not? Because the Web is growing all the time, even changing from one second to the next. Megadirectories try to keep up with the growing World Wide Web, but the

Web always seems to have a jump on them. Plus, there is no central Web registry. Anyone can put a Web page or site out there, but sometimes nobody knows about that page or site. So you can see why a lot of sites just kind of float around in cyberspace without being listed in a directory.

Not all directories want to index the entire Web anyway. Some directories only index sites related to a certain topic. A directory that just indexes sites about sports wouldn't be the place to search for the history of the United States. Others only want to index what they think are the best Web sites, and not all Web sites make the cut.

Nearly all directories offer a keyword search option. At these sites, you can search category levels to find the topic you are looking for or even search the whole Web using your keywords. Some directories let you choose a category or subcategory first and then search only within that section. This is a great way to narrow your search so you don't get too many unrelated sites listed from your search.

Search Engines

If you know exactly what you are looking for, a search engine may be for you. Instead of browsing through layer after layer in a megadirectory, keyword searches in search engines take you right to your information.

We'll take a close look at how to make good searches on pages 46–61. First, let's get the basics on some of the Web's most popular megadirectories and search engines.

AltaVista. Imagine searching through over 200 hard drives to find a file . . . in less than one second! That's what an AltaVista search does. AltaVista is a search engine that lets you search with one word, a few words, or a question. Just type the words you want to search for and click "Search" to get results. Your results (also called "hits") are ranked so that your closest matches appear at the top of the list. You can also browse around categories at AltaVista if you want to. AltaVista's address is http://www.altavista.com. (For more on AltaVista, see page 54.)

Excite. This search engine is very easy to use. Excite only goes three levels deep, so you won't end up digging through an endless pile of levels. Excite reviews each site in its directory, so you get a short description of each site. Like Lycos (see page 38), Excite doesn't try to index all the sites on the Web—only the ones that they think are the best. Most keyword searches return only sites that contain the words that you requested. However, Excite also finds related terms. For example, if you search for "dog care," you will get a list of sites that feature those two words in their descriptions. But Excite will also bring you pages about "pet grooming," even if the words "dog" and "care" aren't on the page. Get excited by Excite at http://www.excite.com. (For more on Excite, see pages 54–55.)

HotBot. HotBot prides itself on offering an up-to-date list of Web sites (lists like this are also called a "database"). HotBot reviews over 110 million Web pages and sites every three to four weeks. Its database is constantly updated. HotBot is really good at helping its visitors find exactly what you are looking for. HotBot is a really hot spot and can be found at http://www.hotbot.com. (For more on HotBot, see pages 55–57.)

Infoseek. This is another search engine that has a selected directory (it chooses only the best stuff). Infoseek was one of the first search engines to search not only the Web, but also newsgroups and all of the phone books and e-mail directories in the United States! The Infoseek Directory has links to over 500,000 of "the best pages on the Web." Seek out Infoseek at http://www.infoseek.com. (For more on Infoseek, see page 57.)

Lycos. The Lycos megadirectory is far smaller than Yahoo! (see below). The folks at Lycos like it that way. They claim to offer links to only the most popular sites on the Web (the top 10 percent). Lycos has a brief description of each site. This can be really helpful. Lycos also supports keyword searching. Folks can find Lycos at http://www.lycos.com. (For more on Lycos, see pages 57–58.)

MetaCrawler. MetaCrawler is a little different than other search services. This one doesn't have a database. When you search MetaCrawler, it may send your request to several different search engines. MetaCrawler uses most of the search tools listed here, including AltaVista, Excite, Infoseek, Lycos, and Yahoo! MetaCrawler takes your search results and then organizes and ranks them for you. Crawl (or run) to MetaCrawler at http://www.metacrawler.com. (For more on MetaCrawler, see pages 58–59.)

Snap. This search engine is sponsored by the television network NBC. This site looks a lot like Yahoo! (see below). It's set up as a megadirectory, with categories, subcategories, and many, many links. Snap rates sites and puts checks next to the really good ones. Snap also allows keyword searches. See if you think Snap is snappy at http://www.snap.com. (For more on Snap, see pages 59–60.)

Yahoo! Yahoo! is one of the largest, most famous Web megadirectories. It has many categories and a ton of subcategories. Chances are, you can find anything you are looking for here. Yahoo! also lets you perform keyword searches. Yahoo! is waiting for you at http://www.yahoo.com. (For more on Yahoo!, see pages 60–61.)

Yahooligans! Yahooligans! is Yahoo! for kids. Its categories are designed for kids, with choices such as School Bell, Art Soup, and Around the World. It also has a keyword search feature. Every link in Yahooligans! has been checked out and found to be safe for a young audience. This is a great starting point for homework and project help, research, and fun. Hang out

Super Searchers

How do directories and search engines find their sites? These services use Web hunters—sometimes called spiders, worms, or robots—to search the Web for new or updated pages. Each directory has different ways they use to gather information. Sometimes, the same search in different directories will give you identical results. And sometimes the results will be different.

Some categories that seem to pop up in nearly every megadirectory are:

Computers. Hardware and software, downloads, the Internet and Web, computer games . . . pretty much anything related to computers!

Education. K-12 information (look here for homework help), colleges, and other school stuff.

Entertainment. The world of TV, music, movies, and celebrities.

Health. Fitness, nutrition, therapy, medicine, and all kinds of ideas to keep you in (or get you into) tip-top shape!

News. Headlines and full coverage of world, national, and local stories and weather. Features newspapers, magazines, other news services.

Sports (or Recreation & Sports). Pro and minor league sports events, teams, data, and fan clubs.

with Yahooligans! at http://www.yahooligans.com. (For more on Yahooligans!, see page 61.)

Most megadirectories and search engines are pretty simple to use. There are some techniques and tips that can really turn you into a Web-searching pro. We'll get into that a little later on pages 46–61.

Doing good searches can help you avoid a lot of unimportant, dumb, or even harmful material that is on the Web, as we will see in the next chapter. So keep reading and you'll be a Web whiz before you know it!

Chapter 2
"All the News That's Fit to Print"*

The title of this chapter comes from the slogan of *The New York Times* newspaper. This slogan means that the people who work at that newspaper say that they are going to try to print all of the important information that they want people to know about. It also means that if something is not important, untrue, or offensive to the readers, that they won't print it. That's the "Fit" part. That way, people who read the newspaper won't be offended or misled.

However, the World Wide Web does not limit what is put online. Traveling on the Web isn't always a smooth ride. And not all of the information out there is fit to print. Remember that the Web doesn't have anyone overseeing it. A lot of false information gets onto the Web every day. Some people post information that they mistakenly believe is correct. Other untrue information may be put on the Web to intentionally mislead people. Still other sites may have information that is obscene, racist, or otherwise improper.

When using the Web to find information for homework, a project, or for fun, you need to be careful. How can you be sure that the information you find is accurate? The easiest way is to use only respected sites. On the next page you will read about how to tell where a site comes from. The best clue is from a site's title. The site's suffix (.com, .edu, .gov, etc.) tells you a lot about a site. Often, its domain name does, too.

*Copyright © The New York Times. *Permission granted for use.*

You can usually trust information that you get from:

- Educational facilities (.edu).

- Non-profit organizations (.org).

- Sites hosted by established reference materials. For example, Encyclopædia Britannica and Merriam-Webster Dictionary.

- Sites hosted by respected or professional organizations. For example, the National Geographic Society for cultural and wildlife topics or Major League Baseball and the Baseball Hall of Fame for information on baseball history, players, and teams.

- Sites from trusted newspapers and magazines. For example, *Time, Newsweek,* or *The New York Times.* However, keep in mind that some publications may have strong opinions, especially about politics. Sometimes these opinions are written as facts. Read carefully!

When doing projects for school it is always a good idea to get your information from several sources. Don't get facts from just one place and leave it at that. Check out the same information at several respected sites. That's the way real Web research pros do it!

Using Multiple Sources

Taylor is in the fourth grade. His class is learning about biographies. They've already read some biographical books in class. Now, Taylor has to write a biography of a famous person. He decided to write about home run king Mark McGwire. He went online to search for information about Mark McGwire. His search returned several different Web pages and sites that had information on Mr. McGwire.

They were:

- Major League Baseball site: Mark McGwire biography.

- Sports Illustrated site: articles, a biography, and statistics on Mark McGwire.

- ESPN Sports Zone site: Mark McGwire facts, comments, and statistics.

- Biography Online: Mark McGwire biography.

- Gumby's Mark McGwire home page.

- Jimmy's tribute to Mark McGwire.

After checking out all of these pages, Taylor found that a lot of information about Mr. McGwire was the same at each site. Basic information, such as Mr. McGwire's height, weight, birth date, and baseball statistics (including his record-breaking home run total) is the same on each site.

However, some of the sites list some personal things about Mr. McGwire. Jimmy's site lists jelly beans and yogurt as Mr. McGwire's favorite foods. They may be. But no other site lists what his favorite foods are. Taylor can't be sure if jelly beans and yogurt really are Mark McGwire's favorite foods. And, this type of information may not be very important to the biography. Jimmy might have gotten that information from a friend, a magazine article, or maybe he heard it during a St. Louis Cardinal's game. Maybe jelly beans and yogurt are Jimmy's favorite foods or he just made it up. It's impossible to tell.

Therefore, Taylor should not use that information in his biography of Mark McGwire. Taylor should look to the Major League Baseball, ESPN, and Biography Web sites as sources for his report. Personal sites, like those put on the Web by Gumby and Jimmy, can't be trusted and may not be reliable. They don't have the same responsibility to the truth that professional sites do. Gumby and Jimmy may have done great jobs in creating home pages about Mark McGwire. But information on their sites may be incorrect. It may be hard to check as well.

Disinformation

Merriam-Webster's online dictionary (http://www.m-w.com) defines disinformation as: *false information deliberately and often covertly spread (as by the planting of rumors) in order to influence public opinion or obscure the truth.*

Sometimes, people will post data to the Web for their, or their organization's gain. Sometimes, even respected sources, such as popular magazines and newspapers, will publish disinformation without knowing it. Sometimes the truth is hard to find.

You know that lying is wrong. However, some advertisers and organizations do not have a problem with lying to people. That's why it is important to know the sources you use online.

When doing research for school projects or reports, the best way for you to make sure that you are getting honest facts is to use several sources. When Taylor was doing his biography on Mark McGwire, he didn't just use one resource to gather his information. He went to three different respected sources of information and compared what they had to say about Mr. McGwire. The more sources you use to compare information, the better your chances are that the data you use is true.

Web Safety and Cautions

Your parents have taught you to be careful when you're out exploring the neighborhood. They tell you to "Look both ways before you cross the street"; "Only go where you're supposed to"; and "Don't talk to strangers." Some of these wise warnings apply to the Web as well. The Web is just like the real world in a lot of ways. You need to be just as careful in the online world as you are in your neighborhood.

You and your parents will probably want to set some of your own rules about World Wide Web use. Here are some rules that everyone on the Web should follow.

Never give out any personal information. Don't tell anyone your real name, address (street or e-mail), or telephone number. Just like in everyday life, some people can harm kids. Some grown-ups pretend to be kids when they are online, so you have to be extra careful. If you have developed a friendship with someone over the Web, and want to get to know them better, discuss it with your parents first.

Never meet in person with anyone who you met on the Web without your parents' permission. If you have developed a friendship with someone on the Web, and you want to meet in person, have your parents go with you and always meet in a public place. On the Web it is easy for people to pretend to be someone they're not. It is always better to be safe than sorry.

Never send or respond to nasty messages. If you receive a message that disturbs you, show it to your parents. Don't feel bad about reading something upsetting. It wasn't your fault. Just show it to your parents. Nasty messages can be traced to their sender. Of course, you don't want to upset anyone (or get in big trouble), so make sure that you don't send any nasty messages of your own.

Never go where you're not supposed to. The Web can be a magical place. You can see a video of the surface of Mars, talk to kids in other countries, learn about all kinds of things, and play games too. You can also find all sorts of nasty information. Racist, hateful, obscene, and disturbing information is posted on the World Wide Web. If you just go where you are supposed to, every Web experience should be a good one.

You and your parents may talk about some other rules for using the Web. Some rules may include:

- What types of sites you are and are not allowed to visit.

- Time limits for using the computer and going online.

- Participating (or not) in chats.

- Going online (or not) when adults are not home.

All of these **Don'ts** and **Nevers** can be pretty scary. But (here we go again) *don't* worry. Sure, rules aren't meant to be fun. These rules are meant to try and help keep the Web fun— and safe—for you. There are millions of great, safe Web sites out there for you to explore. The Web is a magical open door that is always ready to take you someplace that you've never been to before.

And now that the door is open, let's take a look inside and see what we can find!

Chapter 3
Digging Deeper: Search Techniques

Making good searches on the World Wide Web takes some practice. Just browsing around the Web doesn't require good search skills—and can be a lot of fun. But, when it's time to get to work, you need to know how to find what you need—or at least know how to find the map to get you where you're going! Then it's time to use a search service.

In Chapter 1, we discussed the basics of megadirectories and search engines. We listed the names and main features of some of the most popular ones. Now it's time to really take a look at how to do a good search on the Web. We'll also take a closer look at these megadirectories and search engines.

But first things first. Let's take a look at what might happen during a typical search.

Samantha's fourth grade class went on a field trip to the zoo earlier today. They had a lot of fun looking at and learning about all of the different animals (Samantha especially liked the beautiful, long-necked giraffe). Now, Samantha's teacher, Mr. Myers, has assigned reports on "Your Favorite Animal From the Zoo" for homework. Samantha decided to write her report about the giraffe. Mr. Myers told the class that their reports should include important facts about the animal's size, appearance, habitat, and diet. Samantha decides to search the World Wide Web for information about giraffes.

The first step in conducting a Web search is getting to the search engine (see pages 54–61). Once Samantha has logged onto her ISP and brought up her search feature, she is ready to enter some keywords to start her search.

This step in the search is very important. The search engine actually hunts through the Web looking for the keywords that you type. Any pages that it finds with that word on it will be part of Samantha's search results.

Samantha enters "giraffe" in the box next to the search button (this box is called the "search field") and clicks "Search." After the computer chugs for a few moments, Samantha sees her results—over 6,000 documents! The results displayed include a gift catalog and a page of giraffe jokes. There are just too many pages listed to go through all of them. Samantha needs to figure out how to make her search more precise in order to get the information she needs to write her report for school.

Samantha's search was too broad. There are a lot of documents on the Web that contain the word "giraffe," but might not have any real, factual information about the animal. Samantha needs to "refine" her search.

Refining a search means that you are trying to be more specific. You don't have time to look through 6,000 Web pages to find a few pieces of information! That would take a really long time. You'd be turning in your homework weeks after it was due and your eyes would be as big as saucers from staring at the computer screen for so long! There's got to be a better way to get exactly the information that you need. Fortunately, there is!

Keywords Solve the Mystery

Keyword searching is quick and easy. Just type a word and hit "Search." But it is best when you know—or have a good idea—exactly what you're looking for. Sometimes it takes a couple of tries, using different keywords, to find the correct information.

It's kind of like fishing. You are looking to catch a catfish. So you set the hook up with some bait and throw it in the water. A few moments later the bobber stirs! You have a fish! But it's a tiny goldfish. No good. You take the fish off the hook and throw it back into the water. Maybe next time, you'll use different bait or a lure to attract the catfish. Then, once you use the right bait and fishing technique and catch a catfish, you might decide that this fish is too small. You need to catch a three-pound catfish.

In Samantha's search, the keyword "giraffe" was too broad. With keyword searching, you can tailor the search so you get exactly what you want. Samantha doesn't want just any information about giraffes. She wants to get information about the animal's size, appearance, habitat, and diet.

When a search engine goes to work, it compares exactly what you type to its entire index of Web sites. As smart as computers are, they can only do just what you tell them. A search engine couldn't possibly know that Samantha meant that she just wanted information about giraffes' size, appearance, habitat, and diet.

Choose your keywords carefully. Before you even sit down at the computer, think about your topic. Write some words on a piece of paper that describe what you're trying to find. Then, when you do your search, don't freak out if at first you get a ton of hits. Take a look at your list and use some specific words to make your search better. You can also use words and symbols known as "operators" to make more specific searches.

Operators

Operators are words and symbols that tell a search engine how to treat your keywords. They are sometimes called qualifiers or Boolean operators (see page 50 to read about George Boole, who this term is named after). Operators are very simple, everyday words such as *and, or,* and *not.* Using these words along with your keywords can make Web searches even more specific.

Or. Using "or" between two keywords tells a search engine to find everything that contains either word. Suppose you are studying holidays in school and need to get some information about Chanukah. You know from the lesson at school that Chanukah can be spelled either as "Chanukah" or "Hanukkah." You want to be sure that you get all sites about the holiday in your search results. Therefore, you should type "Hanukkah or Chanukah" in the search field. Usually "or" makes for a very broad search—and a lot of hits. However, if you are having trouble finding any hits, using "or" between a few keywords might do the trick.

And. Using "and" joins your keywords at the hip. You won't get any hits unless both keywords are in the Web site. Some search engines let you use the plus sign (+) for "and." The "and" operator is a great way to narrow your search results. In Samantha's case, she could narrow her search by trying the keywords "giraffe and habitat." The next time you get way too many hits for a search, add "and" plus another keyword.

Not. Using "not" between two keywords tells the search engine to look for the first word but specifically *not* the second one, such as "giraffe not jokes." The search engine will reject any Web sites or pages containing that second keyword. Some search engines let you use the subtraction symbol (-) to mean "not." Using "not" is another way to narrow your search when you get too many hits.

Boolean Searches

Often, World Wide Web searches are called Boolean searches. Why? What does Boolean mean anyway? Is it some kind of skinny ghost?

A Boolean search is one that combines keywords with words called operators such as "and" and "or." The name for these types of Web searches comes from George Boole. He was a mathematician who lived in England in the 1800s. He developed a type of thinking called symbolic logic, which led to a lot of modern math. Symbolic logic used mathematical symbols, such as + and -, in logic. Using these symbols made the equations easier to understand. They helped to get rid of any confusion. Boolean searches use operators the same way. That's why his name is used to describe this way of searching on the Web.

Quotes (""). Putting quotes around any keywords tells the search engine to look for these words exactly as you typed them. Using quotes helps when you're searching for a specific name or phrase because it keeps the words together. For example, if you're looking for information about the American Cancer Society, type "American Cancer Society" in the search box. This way only sites specifically mentioning the American Cancer Society will be in your results. Otherwise, you'll have to sift through millions of sites that have either the words American, cancer, or society in them.

Asterisk (*). An asterisk used in a keyword search is called a "wildcard." You can put the wildcard at the front or end of any word. Use the wildcard if you aren't sure about the spelling of a word in your search. However, try to get as close to the spelling of the word as you can. Don't oversimplify! Say you're looking for information on the Internal Revenue Service. However, you don't know how to spell it correctly. So you type "inter*" into the search field. Wow! That returned millions of hits! It would take a long time to find the Internal Revenue Service in that list. A better way to use the asterisk would be to enter all of the words you do know how to spell into the search field. Then use the wildcard with any word that you are unsure about, such as "internal reven* service."

Parentheses (). These work in searches just like in math. Keywords in parenthesis are kept together and handled before any keywords not in parentheses. Any keywords that you put in parentheses will be considered more important than other keywords you use.

Another helpful hint is to always use capital letters when using operators. That's how search engines know that they are operators and not just other keywords. Most search engines, but not all, understand keyword operators. Some build any usable operators into drop-down menus for easy use. Others will have search "options" or "advanced search" listed next to the search field box. All of these ways to make a search more specific will help you use your time on the Web more wisely.

Search engines have been getting easier to use in the last few years. Some can even answer actual questions. In the future, operators might become outdated. However, for now they're an easy way to make better searches. Look at each search engine's Help features for information and help on searching. We'll discuss the features of each search engine in detail later in this chapter.

Digging Through the Megadirectories

As we pointed out in Chapter 1, nearly all search services have directories. Use directories when you are just browsing through a topic. Some of the information that you find will not surprise you. However, the fun part of using directories is taking a look at the stuff that you didn't expect.

Digging through the levels of a megadirectory is like following clues to buried treasure. Suppose that you are taking the President's Physical Fitness Test in gym class. This national program takes a look at the benefits of exercise. You get interested in this topic and decide to look for more information online. If you decide to look in a megadirectory, your search would go like this.

1. Open your search service. You will probably want to use a service that has a good directory such as AltaVista, Excite, Infoseek, Lycos, Snap, Yahoo!, or Yahooligans!

2. You will see a list of topics. Look them over and pick a few that might have information on the benefits of exercise. Our first choice should probably be Health. Other possibilities might be Lifestyle, Kids & Family, Sports & Recreation, or Hobbies & Interests.

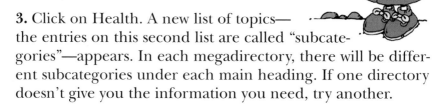

3. Click on Health. A new list of topics— the entries on this second list are called "subcategories"—appears. In each megadirectory, there will be different subcategories under each main heading. If one directory doesn't give you the information you need, try another.

4. Scroll to the bottom of the subcategories. Under this list you might find links to some related Web sites. The pages that these links take you to could have the information that you are looking for. However, not all subcategory lists will include links.

5. Look at the subcategories. Look for topics that will have information on the benefits of exercise. Good choices might be Exercise, Fitness, General Health, or others. Think about your treasure hunt. Are any of these topics clues that will lead you to the treasure?

6. Choose Fitness. Under this subcategory, there might be a lot of sites for gyms and personal trainers that won't help you in your hunt. However, some of the Web sites here look an awful lot like treasure:

What Are These Percentages?

Many search engines rank the sites that they list by using percentile scores. These numbers mean something a little different at each search engine. Generally, if the keyword that you are searching for is in the page's title or comes up often on the page, it will get a high score. However, this number usually doesn't mean very much. A good hit for your search may be around 30 percent. At other times, the 99 percent rating might be right on the money. Don't worry too much about these ratings.

Guidelines for Personal Exercise Programs. This was developed by the President's Council on Physical Fitness and Sports.

Fitness Online. This site brings you continually updated features on nutrition, training, health, fitness, and more.

Shape Up America. Provides the latest information about safe weight management and physical fitness by Dr. C. Everett Koop.

If it turned out that the Fitness subsubcategory wasn't a good choice, you could have used your Back button to move back up to the Health level. Each directory keeps track of the path you follow through its levels. You can see where you've been by looking at this history in one of the pull-down menus at the top of each page (sometimes called "History" or the "Go" menu).

Search Fruitfully

The following megadirectories and search engines were originally mentioned in Chapter 1. These are some of the most popular, useful sites to use when searching for information. Each search service has neat features that make it different than the others. Try them all to find out which ones you like to use the best.

AltaVista. This site is a powerful search engine with some interesting features. AltaVista also has a searchable index. Its index has over a dozen categories for you to check out.

Here are some of the top features you'll see at AltaVista.

- Ask a question! Don't struggle to explain your searches with just a few keywords. Ask AltaVista a question—in plain English (or even another language). Your results page will list the questions that AltaVista can answer first. Usually, these are good matches. Below them will be a list of sites that match any of the keywords in your question.

- AltaVista has a "refine your search" link on the return hits page. Clicking this button brings up a list of topics found on these Web sites. You can refine your search by telling AltaVista to make sure some of the subjects are searched and to keep out others. This is a great feature that will help narrow your searches.

- Using lowercase keywords will return the most hits. If you type "paris" in the search box, AltaVista will return any matches for Paris, paris, or PARIS. If you search for "Paris," AltaVista will only search for Web sites with the uppercase "Paris."

Excite. This site's home page sure offers a lot of services. The search engine and directory indexes are found at the top of the page. Other features include news, sports, finance . . . even your local weather forecast. You can personalize Excite so that when you open it to search you'll see only the news and information that you want to see. Excite will even find local events such as concerts, sports events, and shows for you. Sign up as an Excite member to take advantage of these services. This is free but be sure ask your parents before subscribing to any services.

Here are some of this site's exciting features.

- The Excite directory lists over 20 popular categories of Web sites. Clicking on each category brings up a list of subcategories—which Excite calls departments—and more. You'll also find news headlines, chat rooms, bulletin boards, and related readings on your topic. Check out the Education category. You'll find a K-12 department that features a section devoted to homework help.

- One of the best search features on the Web is Excite's Intelligent Concept Extraction (or ICE). This feature lets you type your search words the same way you would speak. That way, you don't have to think a long time about keywords and operators.

- At the end of each hit on the search results page is a link that lets you search for other pages like that one. This is handy when you find a good match. You can tell Excite to look for more sites just like it.

- At the top and bottom of your results page, you'll find the Search Wizard. The Wizard suggests keywords to help narrow your search. Simply check the boxes next to the words you want and click "Search Again."

- The Power Search feature offers you a variety of search options. These options are in pull-down menus. Without ever typing a Boolean operator you can include and exclude words and phrases.

HotBot. This service is still just a baby in the world of search services. It was born in 1996. HotBot is pretty proud of its up-to-date index. HotBot's entire index is reviewed every three to four weeks. Chances are, you won't get many "the page you are requesting is not found" errors using HotBot (which means that the page no longer exists).

Even though it is young, HotBot has some hot options.

- HotBot's search page is easy to understand and use. Pull-down menus let you customize your search with operators. The first search options window tells HotBot how you want it to treat your keywords—to look for all or any of them or to treat the words as a phrase. You can even tell HotBot: to look for a page's title; to search for a person's name; or that you've entered a

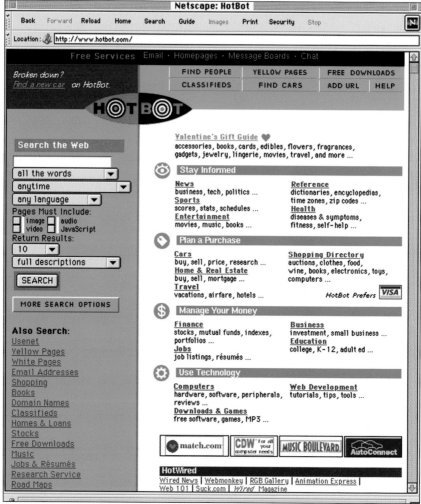

HotBot's home page has loads of search options.

Boolean phrase. Tell HotBot how far back in history to look for your keywords and what language to search in.

- Click the "More Search Options" button for a dizzying list of options. Specify dates, domains (the name of the site's sponsor), and continents of origin—even features such as video—that sites must have. You can even ask HotBot to use "word stemming." This means that if you request a search for "think," HotBot will return pages with "thought" and "thinking" as well.

- HotBot's directory is broken into four categories: Stay Informed (news and other stuff), Manage Your Money, Plan a Purchase (shopping), and Use Technology.

Infoseek. This search engine's directory has been selected—it features only the best stuff on the Web. One big bonus with Infoseek is that it not only searches the Web, but also newsgroups, and all of the phone books and e-mail directories in the United States! The Infoseek Directory has links to over 500,000 of "the best pages on the Web."

- Infoseek Search lets you use regular language for searches (no need to bother with the Boolean operators). You can also search for the answers to questions.

- Infoseek's search results page: lists the path to follow in the directory to get to your requested information; lists matching Web sites; and suggests a few possible areas of interest related to the search.

- Extra Search Precision helps you make very exact searches. It is best used when searching with only one or two keywords.

- Use the "search within these results" option on the search results page to narrow your results.

Lycos. The Lycos home page is an information clearinghouse! Lycos doesn't claim to have the biggest index of all World Wide Web pages, just the best. All pages Lycos links to have been reviewed by Lycos and judged to be useful, interesting, or cool.

- Lycos lists about twenty popular directory categories on its home page. Click on any category and you'll see a page that looks like a magazine's table of contents. The Education category, for example, lists subcategories, such as Areas of Study, Reference, K-12 Schools, and Colleges. You can click on any of these to continue digging through the directory.

- Other nice features under the Education directory category are Today's Feature, Worth a Read, and the Top 5% Education Websites. Looking for homework and project help? Check out Areas of Study in the Education category. From there you can choose your subject or post a message.

- To make a search, type your keywords and hit Go Get It! Lycos Pro Search, in the Search Options section, lets you select several options. One handy feature is the Natural Language Query. This lets you ask a question in plain English (no need for keywords or Boolean operators). Just be sure to select Natural Language Query from the pull-down menu.

- On the search results page, Lycos lists resources that are related to each hit. This gives you the option to visit related sites with a click. Links might be for pages by the same company or about similar topics. Lycos also lists matching categories at the top of your results.

MetaCrawler. Unlike some search engines, MetaCrawler doesn't have its own index of the Web. It sends your search to several other search services such as AltaVista, Excite, Infoseek, Lycos, and Yahoo! MetaCrawler asks these other engines to find hits and then organizes them for you. This makes MetaCrawler a little slower than other search engines. But the way that it is set up gives you a very complete search.

What Are We Searching Here?

Where are search engines really searching? Do they search the *whole* Web? Not really. Each engine has its own list of sites. When you ask for a search, you are only searching that list. Some services, such as Yahoo!, try to have the largest, most complete list. Others, such as Excite, only list the sites that they think are the best. On the other hand, MetaCrawler uses the lists from other services as their list. Sometimes the Web overlaps.

But most search services have their own list of Web sites that they search in. That's why the same search on different search engines will get you different results. Even searching for the same thing on different days using the same search engine can get different results. (Remember that the Web is changing all the time!)

So, when you tell a search engine to search the Web, you're really telling it to search its index of the Web.

MetaCrawler is very simple to use. Just type in your keywords. Then tell MetaCrawler if it should look for any of the words, all of them, or a phrase. Then click Search. In a few seconds, your results page will appear.

Snap. This fairly new search service is produced by NBC and claims to be "creating a search engine as big as the Web itself." That's quite a statement—the Web grows every day!

Here are some services you can use for searching at Snap:

- Just like Yahooligans! and Yahoo!, Snap has shortcut links for each topic. Clicking on these takes you to Snap's most popular subdirectories.

- Some Snap topics have channels. Look for a red link next to the topic. These take you to Snap services. Some channels you'll find include Snap's Inside Entertainment and Travel Planner.

- Snap newsletter gives you the latest info on Snap. This newsletter is free and can be delivered to you through e-mail. Just go to About Snap and fill in your e-mail address. Of course, you should ask your parents first.

Yahoo! This is the biggest directory on the Web—and it grows every day! This is both good news and bad news. The good news is that you can find almost anything you want in Yahoo! The bad news is that you may need to dig through a lot of junk to find it. Use these Yahoo! tips to help you dig faster.

Yahoo! works just like Yahooligans! There is just a lot more information in Yahoo! The tips for using Yahoo! and Yahooligans! are the same.

- Look under each main category link on the Yahoo! home page. See those links? Those are shortcuts links. They link to the most popular subcategories in Yahoo! Clicking on these links takes you directly to that subcategory page. That way, you save clicks and get to browse third-level categories and links right away.

- Searches in Yahoo! are usually pretty good, so you may never need to play around with the search options. If you're curious, select the Options link next to the keyword entry box to see your choices. Here you can tell Yahoo! where to search for your keywords, such as to search only Yahoo! or Usenet (newsgroups).

- After entering keywords and selecting Search, you'll see the Yahoo! search results page. Yahoo! compares your search request to its own directory. The first items Yahoo! returns to you are any matches you had to any of the Yahoo! categories. To get a category match, all of your keywords must be in that category. Often, these categories will have links to sites that are related to your search. Other times, they will have just a word in common, and nothing else. Yahoo! will then list any sites that match your keywords. Above the sites, you'll see links to their categories.

- Links to other search engines are located conveniently at the bottom of each page.

Yahooligans! This site is a searchable, browsable Web directory (like all of the others). But the cool part of this service is that it's especially designed for kids! All of the stuff in Yahooligans! has been checked out and approved especially for young Web users. That way you will get a manageable number of sites to explore in each topic, and you don't have to worry about stumbling onto a site that wasn't meant for kids. Yahooligans! is a great first stop for any school-related project. Remember that all of the hints and tips listed for Yahoo! also work with Yahooligans!

Keep on Seeking!

The more you work with these search services, the better you will get. At first you may think that you are on a wild goose chase. Searching the Web can be hard. But if you follow these easy hints and tips, and keep at it, you'll be a super Web sleuth sooner than you expect! Sometimes people really can find a needle in a haystack—if they have the knack and a plan of attack.

In the next chapter we will take a look at how to become a better student in general. Now that we have the Web basics down, we need to make sure our study habits and school skills are up to par. Then we will finally be able to put all of our new Web skills to good use. Using the World Wide Web to help with school work really can be fun. After a while, you might even forget that you're actually doing schoolwork!

Chapter 4
Study Skills and Test Taking

Learning to study is a lot like learning how to ride a bike. It takes a while and a lot of practice. And sometimes you fall down and scrape your knee. But don't get discouraged. Once you're a good bike rider—or student—you just keep getting better. A good bike rider, like a good Web surfer, can go a lot of places and learn new things. The same is true of learning how to study and take tests.

This chapter doesn't have much to do with the Web, but it will help you become a better student. Just like you can't put a roof on a house before the walls are up, you can't use the Web to help you in your schoolwork until you have the basics of being the best student that you can be! Learning how to be a good student, just like working on the World Wide Web, is best taken one step at a time.

Learning Styles

Being aware of how you learn the best will help you study, and eventually, take tests better. We don't all learn the same way! Which way do you think that you learn things?

Visual learners. These type of students learn something by seeing it. If you're a visual learner, once you see or read information, you'll probably know and remember it.

Aural learners. "Aural" means "of or related to the ear." This type of student learns things better by hearing them. If you're an aural learner, once you hear information, you'll probably remember it. Aural learners can listen to a teacher's lecture and remember and understand what they have said.

Verbal learners. These people need to say information out loud to remember it. Reciting homework and lessons is very helpful to verbal learners.

Lexicographic learners. Boy, that sounds fancy! These people are drawn to written language. They need to write stuff down in order to learn and should always take really detailed notes.

Try to pay attention and see how you learn the best. Think about your vocabulary words. Do you need to read the words and definitions to learn them? Can you remember them after you or the teacher has read them out loud? Maybe you need to write them down in order to understand them.

Being aware of how you learn best can make studying easier. Try these styles and see how they work for you. One style might be just right, or you might try a combination of styles.

Getting Organized

You can't learn to ride a bike or go online without the right equipment. It's the same with studying. For bike riding, you need a bicycle, a helmet, pads, patience, and so on. You need to have the right tools for studying success, too.

Organization is important. It will be pretty hard to do your homework if:

- You don't remember what the assignment is.
- You leave your books at school.
- You aren't sure about what you should do for the assignment.
- You brought home the wrong papers.
- Your books or other materials have been misplaced.

Let's look at some simple organization tools and tips that will help improve your study habits.

Go Home Folder. Keeping a "Go Home Folder" will help you keep your assignments organized. Use a sturdy, two-pocket folder—plastic is best so that it won't be ruined if it gets wet. Mark the left side pocket as the "To Do" pocket. Put any homework worksheets there. You'll also keep your "Assignment Log" there. (We'll talk about that in a minute.) Put anything that needs to go home in your To Do pocket: permission slips, notices for Mom and Dad, or anything else that needs to go home with you. That way, before you leave school, you only need to check one place to see that you have everything. Label the right side of the folder "Done." Put finished homework, signed permission slips and tests, and anything that has to go back to school in the Done pocket.

Assignment Log. Keep a small notepad in your Go Home Folder to serve as your "Assignment Log." In each class, write down any homework assignments in your Assignment Log. Before you go home, check your Assignment Log and make sure that you have any materials that you need for each task in your folder or book bag.

Assignments Calendar. Keep this in your study place at home. Or, you might want to keep this reminder in a family-use area, such as the kitchen, where both you and your parents will see it. Mark down any long-term projects—like reports—in your "Assignments Calendar." Then, break up the assignment into chunks. For instance, you could divide the project into steps such as "research," "rough draft," and "final draft." Mark due dates for those steps on your assignments calendar. That way, these jobs will become part of your homework routine. You won't be pressured at the last minute to do the whole thing (which isn't any fun).

Kory is a sixth grader. She is a smart girl, but her grades aren't very good. Kory and her parents and teachers are sure that she could easily earn better grades. When she does her homework, it is usually done well. However, she forgets to bring some of her assignments home almost every day. Last week, she didn't hand in a social studies report on time because she forgot that it was due. Her locker and book bag are really messy. Often, she loses papers and can't find anything quickly. Her guidance counselor suggested using a Go Home Folder, an Assignment Log, and an Assignments Calendar to help her keep track of her homework.

Kory and her mom bought a folder, an assignment pad, and a calendar. They set up the Go Home Folder and put the Assignment Log in it. They hung the Assignments Calendar in the kitchen on the refrigerator.

After two weeks of using her new organization system, Kory was making progress. Every school day, she would write her homework for each subject on her pad. Then she put any handouts in the folder to bring home. At home, long-term assignments, such as her science project on the water cycle, are listed on the calendar. Kory didn't become a perfect student overnight, though. Sometimes she would forget to bring the Go Home Folder home. But that doesn't happen very often anymore. And her grades are getting better already! Kory says she feels as if school is easier now.

Study Environment

Some kids think that they can (and too often, do) study anywhere: on the floor of their bedroom with music blasting; at the kitchen table, surrounded by brothers and sisters scarfing snacks and talking on the telephone; or sprawled out in the living room with the TV on. . . . Sorry kids—it won't work. Research shows that a good study environment is very important to your success in school.

Let's take a look at your study environment. Do you:

- Study in one regular location designed for studying?

- Study in a place free from noise and interference (TV, loud music, talking, people doing other things)?

- Study in a well-lit place free from visual distractions (posters, TV, pictures, or hobbies)?

- Study in a comfortable (but not too relaxed) place?

- Have all of your study materials in your study location?

You should answer "yes" to all of these questions. Studying in one set place helps you work. Just like your mind knows that it's time to sleep when you're in bed, if you have a usual study spot, your mind will get into a "study mode" when you are there. You will be able to study better.

Noise and visual distractions will hurt your studying. If you study in your room, close the door to block out noise. Leave the TV and your brothers and sisters on the other side. Make a "Do Not Disturb" sign and hang it on your doorknob. Visual distractions should be moved out of sight. You don't want to be looking right at anything that might take your attention away from your studies. Your chair, desk (or table), and light should be just right, so that you are comfortable and can see well, but so that you don't really notice them. Your study area should sort of blend into the rest of the room and feel natural—  no distractions—so that you can focus on your work.

Keeping your study area organized means that you can get right to work—and be finished faster. You should always have just what you need when you are studying.

Keep these important supplies on hand:

- Paper (wide-ruled)
- Pens and pencils
- Ruler
- School notebooks
- School folders
- Reference materials (such as a dictionary, thesaurus, and encyclopedias)
- Calculator

Set goals for yourself to improve your study environment. Remember that nobody can become a perfect student overnight. Just take it one step at a time. If you really try to improve your study area and start studying better, you will see an improvement at school.

Kory used to study on the living room floor. She liked to watch her after-school television program and have a snack while doing her homework. Sometimes, Kory would get too interested in what was on TV, and she would just stop studying. Other days, she would keep working while she watched TV, but it would take a long time—too long.

The TV and her brother and sister constantly interrupted her. Kory was tired of spending so much time on her homework. She began to really dislike schoolwork. And Kory's teacher didn't like the crumpled pages Kory was handing in for homework. Sometimes they had doodles on them. Sometimes they even had crumbs and spills from Kory's snack.

Kory's parents decided that her desk in her room was a better place for doing homework. Now, after school, Kory comes home, eats her snack in the kitchen, and then goes to her room to do homework. She and her parents have set up a good study area in her room. And, since Kory doesn't want to miss her television program, she sets up the VCR to tape it while she studies. Then she watches the program later, after her homework has been finished (and she can fast-forward through those annoying commercials!).

Her desk is against a wall that doesn't have any posters or pictures on it. She tries to keep her desk neat and stocked with supplies. She also decided to move her Assignments Calendar from the kitchen to her new study area. And she is only allowed to listen to quiet music during study time (she likes to listen to soft music that doesn't have any words while she studies—sometimes she even forgets that it is playing). Kory has found that it takes her a lot less time to do her homework. And it seems easier, too, now that she can concentrate better. Best of all, Kory's grades are continuing to go up!

Taking Good Notes

When sitting in class or reading a book for school, it is very important to know how to take good notes. That way, you have a record of important ideas that you can look at later to help in studying. Or, if you forget something that the teacher said, you can always look at your notes to see what you forgot.

We take notes in order to:

- Have a written record to review.

- Force us to pay attention.

- Organize the speaker's words or the text you are reading.

- Have a summary of a classroom discussion or book and to practice lexicographic learning (see page 63).

It's a fact that most people forget half of what they hear or read within one hour! Taking notes is important.

Taking notes is something that you will probably do for the rest of your life. You will continue to use note taking in high school and college. Plus, when you grow up, you may want to take notes at a meeting at work, for a community organization, or a club. The note-taking skills that you develop now will last a lifetime.

So, how do you take good notes? There are several techniques for taking notes. One of them may work well for you. It is important to remember to take notes in a way that works for you—don't just take notes the way your best friend does. You might even come up with a method of your own!

Outlining

When you use an outline to take notes, you list main ideas and put details under them. This breaks up important points so that you can look at them more closely.

Mapping

Mapping is a graphic way of taking notes. It is making a picture to explain the topic. For example, if your map was an apple tree, the topic would go on the trunk, branches would be the main ideas, and the apples hanging from the branches would be the supporting details. Lots of pictures can be used for mapping. See if you can think of any.

Venn Diagram

This is named after John Venn, the English mathematician who came up with the idea. A Venn diagram is used to compare and contrast information. Use it to study any two people, places, or things. A Venn diagram is made of two (sometimes more) intersecting circles. Label each circle for one

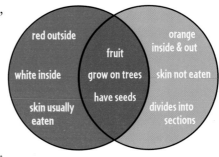

red outside

white inside

skin usually eaten

fruit
grow on trees
have seeds

orange inside & out

skin not eaten

divides into sections

Apples   **Oranges**

of the two things you are comparing. Everything that both things have in common goes in the center section, where both circles meet. The characteristics that describe only one of the things that you are comparing or contrasting goes on the side labeled for that one.

Clues

Always listen closely to what the speaker is saying. These clues will let you know when something important is coming.

- Anything the teacher tells you to write down should be in your notes.

- Anything the teacher writes on the board during a lesson should be in your notes.

- Anything the teacher repeats should be in your notes. Listen for words such as "again," "in other words," and "to repeat."

- Anything the teacher emphasizes should be included in your notes. Listen for words such as "the most important," "remember that," "pay particular attention to," and "the main idea is."

- Examples should be included in your notes to explain a point. Listen for words such as "for example," "such as," "like," and "for instance."

- During the summary, make sure that you have noted all of the important points. Listen for words such as "in conclusion," "to sum up," and "as a result."

Reading Effectively

Reading your textbooks can be hard. With pages and pages to read, sometimes you might forget the beginning before you get to the end. A method called SQ3R can help you get the most out of your reading time. SQ3R stands for Skim, Question, Read, Recite, and Review.

Let's take a look at how SQ3R works.

Skim. First, skim what you are going to read. This means that before reading the assigned text, you should go through it and take a quick look at what you will be reading about. This gives you an overview of the reading. Pay attention to:

- Chapter and section headings
- Introductions
- Sidebars
- Charts and tables
- Picture captions
- Summaries
- End of chapter questions

Question. It is a good idea to question what you read. As you read, make each chapter title and heading into a question. Jot the question down in your notes. As you read, look for the answers to your questions. Pay careful attention to the main points and ideas as you read. The questions will give you a good idea what to look for.

Read. As you read, make sure to look for the aswers to any questions you had. Make a note of anything that you don't understand as you are reading. Look up unfamiliar words in the dictionary. Never be afraid to ask questions. Chances are that you aren't the only one in the class who doesn't understand a difficult concept. Be brave and ask any questions that you have. By doing so, you not only help yourself to learn, but the rest of the class as well!

Recite. Try to say the answers to the questions you had from memory (without looking at the answers!). Think about other examples of similar topics related to your question. This will help you remember the answers in the future.

Note Taking Dos and Don'ts

Do have two pens for taking notes. Ink is easier to read than pencil. You'll have an extra pen if one runs out of ink.

Do use wide-ruled paper and skip a line between each point. This leaves plenty of room to add details later (so have plenty of paper on hand).

Do label the page with the subject and date.

Do tune in to the speaker.

Do ask questions if you don't understand.

Do write down main ideas.

Don't try to write every word your teacher says.

Don't worry about handwriting—as long as you can read it.

Review. When you are finished, review what you have read. Go over it either in your mind, out loud, or on paper. Try to summarize the material (list all of the main points). Review the questions you wrote down and be sure that you know the answers. Go back and reread any points that aren't clear.

Active Study Strategies

How do you usually study? If you're like most students, you look over your notes or reread the textbook. Unfortunately, these study strategies often lead to boredom and daydreaming—even dozing! Study strategies that require action also require attention. Don't let studying be a bore! Some active study strategies include:

Reciting

- Explain the topic out loud and in your own words.

- Teach a lesson on the topic to someone else.

- Ask and answer questions that might be on a test about the topic out loud.

Writing and Remembering

Make and use a set of flash cards for anything that you need help remembering.

- Write the question on one side of the card and the answer on the other.

- Try to answer the cards out loud.

- As you go, make two piles of cards: one for cards you do know and one for the cards you don't know yet.

- Keep going over the cards you don't know, saying the answers out loud.

- Go over the entire pile again to make sure you know them all.

Visualizing

- Close your eyes and picture what you are trying to remember.

- Create pictures and charts to describe what you are learning.

- Go online and visit Web sites about the topic you are studying. You can find pictures, maps, charts, and more online.

Try all of these techniques and see what works for you. Different people need to study differently. The trick is to keep trying until you find a system that works for you.

Test Preparation

Taking tests can make some kids tense. They worry about knowing the answers to the questions. Even kids who study a lot get worried about tests. But by taking good notes, doing your homework, and reviewing material that will be on the test, you will do fine. And remember: Relax!

To help prepare for tests:

- Listen to what the teacher reviews, and ask what you should study.

- Review your class notes.

- Look over your homework assignments.

- Look at the textbook again, and check out the summaries and important points.

Once you know what to study, get ready for the test!

- Use your study area.

- Hang your Do Not Disturb sign.

- Organize your notes and materials.

Then get to work!

- Review, visualize, and recite your material.

- Test yourself to see what you know.

- Make and use flash cards.

- Study with a friend and test each other.

Test-Taking Pointers

Tests are a fact of life in school. Spelling and math tests, essay exams, college entrance exams—these are all important tests that you will have to take. While preparation and studying are the best ways to get ready for tests, there is more you can do. There are some techniques that will help you score better. Think of this as learning how to take a test. There are general guidelines that you can use when taking any test.

1. As soon as the test papers are distributed, jot down any words, facts, or formulas that you might not remember (on scratch paper if you are allowed to use it).

2. Read the directions very carefully.

3. Skim over the entire test.

4. Now read the test. Answer questions that you know the answers to right away. Circle any questions that you are leaving blank.

5. Go through the test again. This time, work on questions that you left blank the first time.

6. *Do not* change any answers you marked unless you are *absolutely sure* they are wrong. Your first impulse is usually the correct one.

7. If wrong and blank answers are counted the same, guess the answers for any questions that you don't know. However, sometimes wrong answers are penalized. If a blank answer is zero points, but a wrong one is minus one, don't guess.

8. Use any remaining time to review your answers.

Not all tests are the same. Some different types of tests are: true/false, multiple choice, and essay.

True/False Tests

This type of a test can be tricky. Typically, sentences will be listed about topics that you have been studying, and you have to figure out if the sentence is true or false. Use these guidelines when taking true/false tests:

- Mark "true" only if a statement is completely true.

- Mark "false" if any part of a statement is false.

- Words such as "all," "always," "never," "none," "only," "best," and "worst" *usually* make a statement false.

- Words such as "often," "probably," "sometimes," and "usually" *often* make a statement true.

- Do not change your first answer unless you're positive it was wrong.

Matching Tests

This type of test asks you to match the correct word with a sentence or to match two ideas that are similar. When taking matching tests remember to:

- Match the ones you know first and cross them out.

- Go through the others. Eliminate any that are obviously wrong. (Sometimes there are more answers than questions. Remember to count to make sure.)

- See if the last step left you with only one answer. If so, make that match.

- When you have eliminated all of your options, guess.

- Use each item only once unless the directions tell you otherwise.

Multiple Choice

These tests list several answers for one question. Your job is to mark the correct answer. Sometimes this can be tricky! Read each question and answer closely. Keep these points in mind:

- After reading the question, first try to answer the question in your head without reading any of the listed choices. Then check to see if one of the listed choices matches your answer; if so, mark it.

- If you don't know the answer, eliminate any that you know are wrong. Eliminate any silly answers.

- Pick the best answer from the remaining ones.

Essay Tests

Some people really dislike essay tests. Writing your own answer, instead of choosing the answer from a list, can be scary. However, if you have done your studying and stay calm while taking the test, you will do fine. Remember to:

- Read all of the questions and mark the ones that you know the answers to—if you have a choice. Sometimes, for example, you will be asked to write essays for three out of five questions.

- Make an outline or map of the main idea and supporting details.

- Check the clock to make sure you have enough time. Don't use up all of your time on the first question.

- Cover only the points asked for in the question. (Don't write about George Washington as president if the question is asking about his role in the Revolutionary War, which happened before he was elected president.)

- Start with a good topic sentence.

- End with a good summary sentence.

Learning how to take good tests doesn't have to stop after the test is over. After you get a test back, read over any comments carefully. Try to understand any mistakes that you made. Ask your teacher if you have any questions.

Keep at It

Putting together successful study strategies takes time—and some work. Try some of these and see what works for you. The right strategy will make studying easier for you and help your grades and understanding of your schoolwork. And at the same time you are developing good skills that will help you in all kinds of things in your life—including using the World Wide Web!

Chapter 5
Research and Report Writing

Writing a good report requires getting your act together. First, you may need to pick a topic (unless one has been assigned to you). Then you'll have to gather information and make an outline. Writing the rough draft and editing it comes next. Then the final draft can be composed. Also, you may want to find some pictures, charts, maps, or other visual information to jazz up your report. The Web can be a great resource for report writing in several ways.

- You can use the Web to help you pinpoint a topic that interests you.

- Researching on the Web gives you immediate access to a lot of information.

- Hunting on the Web for extra resources will lead you to great clip art, graphics, maps, charts, video and audio clips, and more.

Follow these steps for report-writing success.

1. Choose a topic. First, you will probably select a general topic. Usually, this will be something that is related to the unit you're studying in class. Your general topic might be the American Revolution, space travel, or energy. Many students try to write their reports using these broad subjects. However, a successful report needs to have more of a narrow focus. Better topics would be: the Boston Tea Party or General George Washington; the history of the space shuttle program or Apollo 11's voyage to the moon; or solar energy or making your home more energy efficient.

2. Locate resources. A big part of writing reports is doing research. You need to find good information to include in your report. Of course, the library is a good place to find books, reference materials, and periodicals. Use the Web too. It will give you access to publications your library might not stock. Plus, you get to visit sites for agencies and organizations. What would a report on the history of the space shuttle be like without a visit to NASA and the National Air and Space Museum? Let the Web broaden your horizons. And the information you can find online is often much more current than information in books printed years ago (very appropriate for the space shuttle report!). Remember to mark sites you might want to use in your report as Bookmarks. Make a special folder just for this report and put all your links there. Then you'll be able to find them easily when you're ready to take notes. Plus, if you need to write a bibliography, you'll have a good record of your sources.

3. Take notes. Use the reading techniques we discussed on pages 68–72 to gather information about your topic. Take a lot of notes. It's always easier to leave extra things out later than to try and stretch a skimpy report.

4. Develop an outline. This forces you to organize your notes. You can use the mapping technique we talked about on pages 69–70. Try to find four to seven main points to write about under your main topic. These will be your subtopics. Then, your notes should fit under the subtopics. Make sure each subtopic is just a word or two—a phrase at most. Under the subtopics, write the supporting details and other information. If you're using mapping, make a new map for each subtopic and fill in details from your online and traditional (library) research. If you have some blank spots in your outline, go back online or to the library. (For detailed online search techniques, see pages 46–54.)

5. Write your rough copy. After your teacher has said that you have enough information, sharpen your pencil—or boot up the computer. It's time to write. Your first paragraph is called

How the Web Can Help

If you have a general topic in mind—Energy, for example—see if the Web can help narrow it down. Use a Web site that has a big directory—such as Yahoo! or Excite. Type "Energy" into the search field box and click on its category link. You'll probably see dozens of subcategories there. Some will have information on things that you know about, such as solar power, wind power, or energy efficiency. Other topics may sound pretty weird, such as sonoluminescence, which is—as strange as this sounds—the release of light by bubbles in a liquid that has been excited by sound! (There are several Web sites on this topic, if you're interested.) Browsing around these categories is a great way to find a topic.

the introduction. This is where you tell your readers what the report is going to be about. The main part of the report is called the body. This is where you write about the subtopics. Use each subtopic or map to write a new paragraph. Make sure that you follow your outline. If at any time you think that you need more information, go back online or to the library. The final paragraph is called the conclusion. This should sum up the report and restate why your topic is important.

As you write the rough draft, don't worry about spelling, grammar, or handwriting. Just keep writing. Keep your concentration. Skip lines (or make the copy double-spaced on the computer) so you have room for corrections.

6. Now it's time to edit the rough copy. As you look over your report, ask yourself these questions:

- Is the title of my report interesting?

- Does the introduction explain the title and what the report will be about?

- Does the introduction make readers want to read on?

- Does the body of the report provide detailed information on my topic?

- Does the body do what the introduction said it would?

- Does the report give factual information?

- Does the conclusion briefly sum up the report?

- Does the report give a complete picture of my topic?

You should answer "yes" to each of these questions. If not, go back and make changes to the report. Then reread and check for spelling, punctuation, and grammar.

7. Write your final copy. Be sure to double-check spelling, punctuation, and grammar. Make sure you have included all required parts of the report, such as a title page, charts, bibliography, and anything else that was required. Check neatness! Teachers don't like to read sloppy assignments.

Space Is the Place

Tyrone's fifth grade class has been studying space exploration. Now he needs to write a report on that topic. The class has discussed a lot of different things about outer space. They have learned about the Soviet space program, Alan Shepard's journey into space, the space shuttle program, and even the space station that scientists are planning to build. There is so much that Tyrone could write about that he's having a hard time deciding!

Step 1: Choose a topic. Tyrone's general topic is space exploration. At first, Tyrone was thinking about writing on either the Soviet space program, astronaut training, or Voyager's journey to Mars. Finally, Tyrone decided to do a biography on legendary astronaut John Glenn. When

Mr. Glenn recently joined the crew of the Space Shuttle Discovery at the age of 77, he was in the news a lot. Tyrone watched Discovery's lift-off and landing, and he followed the details of the voyage on television and the Web.

Step 2: Locate resources. First, Tyrone did some brainstorming. He thought of places where he might find information and biographies about John Glenn. After thinking a bit and writing some notes, his list included the library, NASA, and the National Air and Space Museum. Then Tyrone logged onto the Internet and began his initial search for information on John Glenn. His first stop was Yahooligans! Tyrone typed in "John Glenn" in the search field box and hit Search.

Yahooligans! listed several hits for his search: a biography from Mr. Glenn's college; some transcripts from the chat Yahooligans! had with John Glenn while he was in space during his shuttle mission; and several Web sites with pictures and information from Glenn's Mercury days.

Tyrone found a neat site called Ask an Astronaut that was sponsored by the National Space Society. Here, he read John Glenn's answers to questions posted in 1996 as well as a John Glenn biography. At this site, Tyrone could even ask a question for a real astronaut to answer!

Some of the other sites looked helpful as well. The NASA site had a good biography of every astronaut, past and present. The National Air and Space Museum had lots of information on Mr. Glenn's shuttle mission. Tyrone was learning a lot about John Glenn. For instance, Tyrone knew that Mr. Glenn was an astronaut. But he also learned that Mr. Glenn had served in World War II and had also been a United States Senator! Some Web sites that Tyrone visited included:

- NASA Astronaut biographies
  (http://www.jsc.nasa.gov/Bios/index.html)

- NSS Ask an Astronaut (http://www.nss.org/askastro)

• The National Air and Space Museum
(http://www.nasm.edu)

• The U.S. Senate (http://www.senate.gov)

Step 3: Take notes. Tyrone printed out a lot of the pages he found. That way he could make notes right on the pages. First, he skimmed the material quickly. Then, he jotted down headings and subheading to start making his outline.

Step 4: Make an outline. Tyrone used the headings and sub-headings to create main topics for his outline. He used the following topics, in this order, as his main points.

1. Personal information and education

2. Military experience

3. Mercury Space Program

4. Senator John Glenn

5. STS-95 Mission

Then Tyrone found important points to list under each of these headings. These points became subtopics. He then listed his research notes under each of these subtopics. Each subtopic will become a paragraph in his report. He checked his resources for more information whenever he needed to.

For example, under the Senator John Glenn heading, Tyrone listed these subheadings: Elections, Committees, and Sponsored Legislation. Each of these subheadings will be developed into a paragraph in Tyrone's report. In the Committees paragraph, for example, Tyrone will describe each of the four Senate committees that Mr. Glenn served on.

Step 5: Write a rough copy. Now it's time to turn those headings into paragraphs. Before writing anything, Tyrone took his outline into class to get his teacher's approval. Then Tyrone wrote his report using his notes and outline. He wrote quickly and didn't worry about spelling or neatness. He skipped lines, so he could insert more details and make corrections easily. He referred to his outline a lot while writing.

Step 6: Edit the rough copy. Tyrone looked over his report and decided that *Biography of John H. Glenn, Jr.* wasn't a very interesting title. Borrowing some words from NASA Mission Control on STS-95, he changed the title to *An Astronaut Hero and American Legend: John Glenn.* He continued reading over the report and made a few changes to correct mistakes and make it more interesting. He reread it again and corrected spelling and grammar. He even had his mom read the report, and she suggested a few other changes.

Step 7: Write the final copy. Tyrone then typed the final draft of his report on his computer. He was careful not to make mistakes. When he was finished he did a spell check and read the report again. He double-checked the report's punctuation, spelling, grammar, and vocabulary. He had his dad take a look at the final copy as well. Tyrone was excited about what he had learned and how the report had turned out.

Oral Reports

Suppose Tyrone's teacher had assigned an oral report instead of a written report. What would Tyrone have done differently?

Actually, a lot of his preparation would have been the same. He would still have needed to pick a topic and collect resources. He would have had to take notes and develop an outline. He would have used the outline to write a rough draft and then edited that copy before writing a final copy. But instead of just handing in a printed report, Tyrone may have written notes he could refer to on note cards as he gave his oral report in front of the class. Or, he might have created an extended outline to use during his presentation.

When preparing an oral report, you need to be very familiar with your topic. Tyrone has learned a lot about Mr. Glenn while preparing the report. But Tyrone would have to prepare notes to use while he gave the presentation (either on note cards or in the form of an outline). You can't just read a report, word for word, in front of the class. Everyone would fall asleep! He would practice presenting his oral report to some friends or his parents before getting up in front of the class so that he would be used to speaking about his topic in front of people.

Also, Tyrone would have to get some more materials to help involve his classmates in his presentation. Perhaps he would have wanted to distribute handouts or hang some pictures on the chalkboard. Here the World Wide Web really helps Tyrone. At the National Air and Space Museum, he could have found a picture of John Glenn's original space ship, the Friendship 7. At Yahooligans!, he could have found photos to show that were taken of Earth from the window of Friendship 7. Or he could have printed and distributed some of John Glenn's Senate speeches. Remember: Tyrone would have to make sure that all of the visual resources he used from the Web were OK for public use. If you are ever in doubt about the restrictions on a resource, just ask whoever is in charge of the Web site.

The Web is a valuable research tool to use when writing reports and developing presentations. Current information, as well as historical data, is really at your fingertips. And the Web is a great resource for finding cool pictures and other graphics that can dress up your reports. But it is not just a great resource for big projects. It is also a very valuable tool to use when you need help with everyday homework, as we'll see in the next chapter.

Chapter 6
Homework and Other Projects

Homework. What is interesting about homework? You get assignments, you go home, you do them, and you hand them in, right? How could the Web help with homework?

You would probably be surprised at all the homework help waiting for you on the Web. You just need to read the signs and find the right exit on the Information Superhighway. We're going to point out those important signs for you, so keep reading and keep your eyes peeled!

Pretty much every teacher assigns homework, so it must be important. Teachers assign homework to help students:

- Practice new skills that were learned in class. Practice helps you remember what you learned.
- Keep old skills fresh.
- Review what you learned in class.
- Learn new things not covered in class.
- Prepare for new lessons.

Did you know that homework helps teachers too? By assigning homework, teachers:

- Check how well you understand their lessons.
- Discover what areas you need help in.
- Identify areas the class needs to review.

Homework Tips

Before we jump back into the Web, let's go over a few general homework hints that will help you.

Pick a set study time. By doing your homework at the same time every day, your brain learns to get into a "homework mode" then. You probably get hungry and sleepy at around the same times each day. You should study at the same time each day, too.

Make your study time a definite period of time. If you know you have to spend at least 45 minutes in your study area, you won't feel the need to rush through your work. You may want to give yourself a little free time when you first get home to relax and have a snack. Don't wait too long to get to work though. You need plenty of time to do your homework well.

Set up a study area. Remember when we described an ideal study area a few chapters back? Take another look at pages 65–68 to see what a good study area should be like, and compare it to your current study area. Try to make sure your study area is as close to that description as possible. You'll thank yourself (and your teachers and parents will as well!).

Do the hardest stuff first. Early in your homework session, you'll probably have the most energy. This is the time to get the hardest assignments—or ones you like the least—out of the way. Save the assignments you like for last—sort of like homework dessert (like a nice, long division eclair!).

Take a break. You should take a break from the books every 15–20 minutes (I know you can handle this . . .). Stand up and give your body a long stretch. Walk around and maybe drink some juice. When you get back to your desk, you'll have more energy. Your concentration will be back and you'll get more work done.

Ask for help. If you don't understand something, ask your parents or an older sibling to explain it. If that doesn't get you anywhere, check out some of the Web sites that are listed on page 89 and page 91 for help. Sometimes it takes a day or so to get an answer, though. If you get stuck and can't finish your homework on time, don't freak out! Just explain it to your teacher the next day. The most important thing to remember is to really give homework your best shot.

Using the World Wide Web is always fun and interesting. But how can we use it to help with homework assignments? Let's find out! The following sites have all sorts of homework hints and help to give.

Get Responsible!

Even though you're a kid, and you don't really have a "job" (like grown-ups), going to school and doing homework is kind of like your job. It's something that you have to do every school day and even though you have fun at school, you always do some work. Here are some common excuses and solutions for not handing in homework.

Excuse: "My dog ate my homework."

Solution: Keep your homework in your To Do Folder and safely out of the reach of Poochie. Plus, make sure that Poochie has his own food and toys. That way, your vocabulary words won't look so tasty!

Excuse: "I fell asleep before I finished my homework."

Solution: Do your homework shortly after school or early in the evening so you will have enough energy to finish it. You could also do homework at school during any breaks.

Excuse: "I forgot that we had homework."

Solution: Write homework in your Assignment Log and keep it in your To Do Folder. Check the Log before you go home to make sure that you have everything you need.

Excuse: "No one reminded me to do it."

Solution: Homework is part of your job. Take responsibility for remembering it yourself.

The Homework Hotline Online Schoolhouse (http://www.wvptv.wvnet.edu/homework) is actually an interactive television program that helps students with their math and science homework. It also has great online resources for common homework questions in those areas. Click on the schoolhouse and check out the Science lab for some easy and fun at-home science experiments. And if you don't find what you are looking for, simply send your question to the Homework Hotline teachers!

The Alphabet Superhighway (http://www.ash.udel.edu/ash/index.html) is sponsored by the United States Department of Education. This site helps students create, locate, and communicate information through online activities. Some things you'll find at ASH include: active learning, guided discovery, mentoring, and competitions. Smart Searcher helps you find information, either within the Alphabet Superhighway or elsewhere on the Web.

This site has great search tips, too. The Traveling Tutor presents mini-lessons on a variety of topics: how to draw graphs and diagrams, how to write better reports, and more. The Challenge Chaser presents challenges for students to work: essay writing, information searches, spelling words, and word puzzles.

ICONnect's KidsConnect (http://www.ala.org/ICONN/kidsconn.html) is a question-answering, help, and referral service for students. The site is posted by the American Association of School Librarians, a division of the American Library Association. Ask a question at this site and a school librarian will e-mail you an answer. Well, they won't *give* you the answer, but they'll tell you where to find it.

If you're a little intimidated about searching the Web, the librarians at KidsConnect can help you get started. Plus, this site lists nearly 100 favorite sites in all sorts of topics, and most of them are school-related.

Projects

The Web can be a great homework partner. When you're doing projects, you can use the Web for research. You can also use it to get ideas and find stuff—like maps, clip art, recipes, graphics, quotations, and more—to dress up your projects.

The Franklin Institute Science Museum has a *Kids Did This* Web page (http://sln.fi.edu/tfi/hotlists/kids.html). Visit it to see projects produced by kids! It's a great site to get ideas for projects in all subject areas. Sometimes they tell you where the kids who did these projects found their information and graphics.

Ask an Expert

Sometimes when kids get stuck they just want to find somebody who really knows their stuff to answer a few questions. When you are looking for a real pro to help you with something, check out these sites. Most let you choose from a variety of topics.

- **Ask an Expert Page** (http://njnie.dl.stevens-tech.edu/ curriculum/aska.html)

- **Pitsco's Ask an Expert** (http://www.askanexpert.com/ askanexpert/cat/index.html)

- **Ask an Expert** (http://www.askanexpert.com/askanexpert)

There are also tons of sites with access to experts in a variety of subjects. See pages 94–103 for more on expert information on the Web.

Get Original!

The kids in Zach's fourth grade class are writing books for a language arts unit. Zach has selected Italy as his topic. He did

Homework Helper Sites

These are some of the best homework helper sites on the World Wide Web. Pop onto these pages when you are stuck on a homework problem, or even if you are just looking to learn something new!

Internet Public Library (http://www.ipl.org/teen) is a general homework help page that lists a lot of good sites that have links to all kinds of homework help.

Schoolwork Ugh! (http://www.schoolwork.org) is a directory that lists other Web sites by category. It is run by a friendly librarian who will answer your questions by e-mail.

B.J. Pinchbeck's Homework Helper (http://tristate.pgh.net/~pinch13/) has over 530 homework help links and has won over 100 awards. Amazingly, it was put together by 11-year-old B. J. and his dad. According to B. J., "If you can't find it here, you can't find it."

The WKBW Homework Home Page (http://www.wkbw.com/homework/homework.html) includes links to many reference and educational areas.

G.R.A.D.E.S. Archive at Classroom Connect (http://www.classroom.com/Grades/) is a selection of educational Web sites. Some sites are for teachers, but you'll also find sites for students in grades K-6.

some research in his school library. Then, he logged on to the computer to do some research online. He found some additional information about Italy, its geography and history. He also found some great stuff to make his report really original.

Zach started his search at Excite. He opened the Education directory and then went to the Reference subdirectory. He decided to look for maps first. A site called Atlapedia (http://www.atlapedia.com) had some good information. He also found some cool 3-D maps at 3D Atlas Online (http://www.3datlas.com). Zach downloaded some of the maps (see page 95 for information about downloading) that showed Italy's geography and climate, and he even found a real picture of Italy that had been taken from a satellite!

Next, Zach decided to add some common Italian words and expressions to the back of his book. Searching in HotBot, Zach found A Web of On-line Dictionaries (http://www.fac-staff.bucknell.edu/rbeard/diction.html). This site lists over 800 online dictionaries—in over 160 languages! Zach was pretty sure that he could find an Italian-American dictionary here. He actually found several. There's a Beekeeper's Italian-English Dictionary, but Zach didn't really need to know words such as beehive (*alveare*) or swarm (*sciame*). The World Surfari's English-Italian Translator (http://www.supersurf.com/italy/ital-eng.htm) let Zach type in words and phrases and gave him the Italian. "Cool," thought Zach, "just what I need." Interestingly, the search engine giant AltaVista does World Surfari's translations. The World Surfari site also had more information on Italy and its people. Zach printed some pages and made some notes to add to his book.

Everyone loves Italian food, so Zach thought that some recipes would spice up his book. Zach went to Yahoo! and tried to find a category for Italian food. He started in the Society and Culture heading and went down through the Food & Drink and Countries & Cultures subheadings until he finally found "Italian." There, he found several recipe sites. He found a site that listed the recipes to some of Zach's favorite dishes. He decided to include the recipes for tomato sauce, Italian cookies, and (his favorite) stuffed, cheezy calzones. He printed out the recipes to use in his book. He was sure that his teacher and friends would think they were delicious.

Zach wanted to include some famous Italians in his book, but he wasn't sure where to find them. He tried a few search engines without any luck. He thought that Christopher Columbus was a famous Italian, so he searched directory sites—such as Yahooligans! and Lycos—for "Christopher Columbus." He was hoping that one of the hits would lead him to a Web page about famous Italians. No luck there, either. Zach was beginning to get frustrated. Finally, Zach went to KidsConnect and sent an e-mail asking a librarian where to find a list of and information on famous Italians.

The next day, Zach got a response back—from a school librarian in Tokyo! She found some great sites for Zach. First, she told him how she found them. She did a search in AltaVista. She entered "famous + italian" in the search box. She got three good hits from that search. One was the Italian-American Website of New York. Another one listed Italian-American celebrities.

Zach visited all of these sites. He learned that two men who signed the Declaration of Independence were of Italian descent: Maryland's William Paca and Delaware's Caesar Rodney. He also learned that the man who supposedly captured Billy the Kid, Angelo "Charlie" Siringo, was of Italian descent. Italian-Americans invented the one-handed basketball lay-up and the ice cream cone too. Zach learned about Italian-Americans who fought in the Civil War, wrote famous songs, and founded famous companies. The librarians at KidsConnect really came through for Zach! He remembered to send an e-mail message back to the librarian who had helped him to thank her.

Because the World Wide Web has so much information for you to check out, chances are that you will find new stuff all the time. And this will make the research you do interesting—and it will make your work interesting for other people. You can find all kinds of examples to use in projects. This will make the work you do very much your own—chances are, it won't be like any of the other projects in the class!

Chapter 7
Online Reference Resources

Access to reference material is important. Sometimes a search of the World Wide Web isn't necessary when working on school projects. You might just want a quick overview of a subject or some important facts. Or maybe you just need to look up a word, find a map, or find synonyms for a word. When this is the case, using reference materials is your best bet.

These resources help you find information on a variety of subjects. Plus, most reference materials are very reliable and comprehensive. They are probably some of the first places to turn to for information.

- Need help with your vocabulary words? Pull out a dictionary.

- Looking for information on DNA for your science report? Grab the encyclopedia.

- Studying the mountains of Australia? Look in an atlas.

- Writing a paper and need another word for "try" (which you've already used 12 times!)? Get out your thesaurus.

There are a lot of uses for reference materials—both for school and everyday questions. Suppose that your mother swears that your baby brother never sleeps if there's a full moon. Your mom might check a calendar for the next full moon. If your dad is an avid gardener, an almanac is a valuable reference for him. And the telephone directory is one reference book that people use every day.

But buying all kinds of reference books can be expensive. And sometimes you don't have time to go to the library (or would prefer to get your information from home). Luckily, today a lot of popular reference materials are online.

Downloading

After you have been searching the Web for a while, you suddenly come upon the perfect graphic for your project! After making sure that it is OK to do so, you are ready to download it. On most Web browsers, it is pretty easy to figure out how to download a Web page or graphic. Usually, you will pull down the File menu and choose Save As. In Netscape Navigator, the Save As dialog box will automatically figure out what you are trying to save (either text or an image) and will suggest how to save your information.

Then you will just need to choose where on your hard drive you want to keep the file. It is probably a good idea to create "Download" folders for each new project that you work on so you can keep your information organized. And, instead of downloading, you sometimes might want to just print the page that you are on, if you think that you won't need to keep it stored. If that is the case, all you have to do is make sure that you are on the page that you want to print and click the Print button.

Downloading is usually used to save graphics to insert into projects at a later time. Always remember to respect any copyrights that people have assigned to their work. Never take credit for anybody else's work. That's called plagiarism and is another name for stealing. But don't worry. A lot of people on the Web want to share their work, and you can find a lot of cool, free stuff to download.

Now, let's look at some common—and helpful—reference materials that you can find and use online.

Encyclopedia Answers

An encyclopedia is a comprehensive summary of information. Some encyclopedias focus on specific topics. However, most encyclopedias cover all kinds of general information.

Why use encyclopedias on the Web? Encyclopedia volumes on the Web add bells and whistles that you won't find in the books at the library. Just like regular encyclopedias, online volumes have articles with information, but they also feature such extras as pictures, graphs, and maps. Also, encyclopedias on the Web sometimes feature video and audio clips as well as

links to other related Web sites. An online encyclopedia can really be one-stop shopping for information. Remember how heavy those volumes in your library can be? No more weight lifting! When using an encyclopedia on the Web, you just type, point, and click!

More specific online encyclopedias exist on the Web as well. For example, you can check out the Encyclopedia of the Orient. This reference material has information about Far Eastern countries, from Algeria to Yemen. In another encyclopedia, The Encyclopedia Mythica, you can search for information on mythology and folklore from all over the world. Another example of a specific reference source is The Stanford Encyclopedia of Philosophy. This resource covers all you might need to know about philosophers and philosophy.

Online encyclopedias exist for all kinds of specific topics. If you can find one that covers your subject, it can be a great discovery. However, general-purpose encyclopedias are usually good enough sources for help with homework, papers, and projects.

Dictionary Details

Dictionaries are alphabetical listings of words or phrases. They contain definitions and sometimes other information, such as pronunciation, synonyms, where the word came from, and sentence usage.

Online Encyclopedias

Funk and Wagnall's Multimedia (http://www. funk-andwagnalls.com) is part of the Funk & Wagnall's Knowledge Center. This site is absolutely free, but you need to register to use it. Be sure to ask your parents if it's OK first. Once inside, you can search for articles by typing in your topic or by using their directory. Articles are easy to read and full of information.

The Internet Encyclopedia (http://www.clever.net/ cam/encyclopedia.html) may not look very cool, but it's totally free and has *tons* of information. Select the Macro-Reference index to get a list of general topics or Micro-Reference for detailed, specific subjects.

Encyberpedia (http://www.encyberpedia.com/ency.htm) isn't really an encyclopedia. It's more like an encyclopedia directory. Click on any of the subjects in the button bar on the left-hand side of the screen. However, this doesn't give you an article. What Encyberpedia does give you is a definition of the topic and a staggering list of links. Most have detailed descriptions, so you can find just the information you need.

Encarta Online (http://encarta.msn.com) has a condensed version of its encyclopedia that is available for free and gives you good basic information. Most searches will give you several hits. Unfortunately, you have to pay to use the deluxe version of this encyclopedia.

Just like encyclopedias, online dictionaries sometimes jazz up entries. For example, when you look up the word "web" at the WWWebster Online Dictionary, you will find that it is a noun, it came from the Old English word "wefan" (which means "to weave"), and it has various definitions. Sounds a lot like an entry in a regular dictionary, doesn't it? However, this dictionary entry also has links to related words such as "cobweb" and "spiderweb." Learning all about a word can make its spelling and meaning easier to understand—and remember.

Online Dictionaries

WWWebster Online Dictionary (http://www.m-w. com/ dictionary.htm) is considered *the* online dictionary. And it couldn't be easier to use. Just type your word in the dictionary search field and click Search. Not only do you get the word's meaning, but also included is the word's pronunciation, part of speech, and how to change its form (like how to make it plural). Also included are links to entries for similar words. This dictionary even gives you the history and date of creation of the word you look up.

OneLook Dictionaries (http://www.onelook.com) lets you search more than 430 dictionaries at once. Type in your word and hit Search. Then this search engine goes to work consulting 29 general dictionaries, including Webster's and WorldNet Vocabulary Helper, and then gives you a link to each dictionary's definition. You can also request searches of pronunciation and spelling dictionaries, as well as special dictionaries for a particular topic such as medical, business, technological, slang, or sports.

A Web of Online Dictionaries (http://www.fac-staff. bucknell.edu/rbeard/diction.html) provides links to over 800 dictionaries. These dictionaries list words in over 160 languages! You've probably never heard of most of them, but it's fun to take a look. This Web site also has some helpful links to grammar guides (also in a variety of languages) and thesauruses.

Thesaurus Sources

A thesaurus is a kind of dictionary. It lists words with their synonyms and antonyms. Do you ever find yourself looking for a word that's on the tip of your tongue? You can think of similar words, but not the right one. Or what about when you've used the same word over and over again in a paper? You need to find some words that mean the same thing, but can't get that one out of your head. At times like this, reach for a thesaurus—or visit one online.

Online thesauruses are simple to use. Just type in your word and then get a list of words with the same meaning. Online thesauruses are helpful because not everyone owns one. It's not the sort of book most people use every day.

Almanacs Anyone?

Almanac's are books of facts about a certain subject. They are updated and published yearly. Almanacs usually have lists, charts, and tables of information.

Almanacs on the Web are really useful. Since almanacs are annual books, they become outdated quickly. The online versions always offer current information and are often updated more than once a year. The almanac on your family bookshelf at home might be from 1983. The library is probably more up to date with almanacs from 1996, 1997, and 1998, but no 1999! Then it's time to go online for some fresh information.

Online Thesauruses

Roget's Online Thesaurus (http://www.thesaurus.com) is a wonder for Web word searchers. Peter Roget spent over 50 years cataloguing and categorizing words and their synonyms. This online version of Roget's thesaurus is really impressive. First, type in the word that you are requesting synonyms for. If your word is listed in more than one category, you'll be asked to select the general definition that matches your needs. You can also browse the thesaurus alphabetically or by using the six classifications that Roget originally came up with in the early 1800s.

WWWebster Thesaurus (http://www.m-w.com/thesaurus.htm) is part of the Merriam-Webster dictionary site. In this impressive online thesaurus you'll get the Merriam-Webster word definitions in addition to the requested word's synonyms. It's not as extensive as Roget's, but not as overwhelming either.

Online Almanacs

Information Please (http://www.infoplease.com) is almost a reference bookshelf in itself. It has a dictionary, an encyclopedia, and an almanac. To browse the almanac's categories, use the button bar along the left-hand side of the screen. Use the search feature to look in just the almanac or all the reference sections.

The CIA World Factbook (http://www.odci.gov/cia/publications/factbook/index.html) should be your first stop for information about foreign countries. In the Countries section, you are given a list along the left-hand side of the screen to choose from. Once you find the country you are looking for, click on it. The first thing you will see is the country's flag and map. Then all of the country's geography is listed as well as important historical information and current issues. You also get details on the country's people, military, economy, government, transportation, and more. You name it, it's here!

The Old Farmer's Almanac (http://www.almanac.com) has quite a history. The printed version of this online resource has been used since 1792 for weather and planting information. Now you can visit this farmer on the Web. This site is helpful when doing science reports on a variety of topics. Select Site Index from the pull-down menu on the home page and hit Go. You'll find a linked list of topics to choose from, or you can just browse from there.

Get the Facts With an Atlas

An atlas is a collection of maps. Most atlases also give you some geographical information. But these maps tell you much more than how to avoid getting lost!

Atlases on the World Wide Web really jump off the screen. Ever find yourself with your nose to a map trying to read the name of some river or city? Forget about looking for a magnifying glass! On the Web you can just point and click to zoom in on whatever you want.

What if you need more information about something you see on a map in a traditional paper atlas? You would have to find somewhere else to look it up. Online, you can just point and click. Links and more give you plenty of information. And with Web atlases, you don't need to wait to buy the next edition for updated data.

Online Atlases

The National Atlas of the United States (http://www.atlas.usgs.gov/) is easy to use. Its maps give you a bunch of pictures of the United States. Here you can get geographical information as well as facts about different cultures and societies from around the country. You can roam across America and zoom in wherever you want to reveal more detail. Just point at map features with your mouse to learn more about them.

U.S. Census Bureau Tiger Mapping Service (http://tiger.census.gov/) provides high-quality, detailed maps of anyplace in the country. This easy-to-use atlas is especially good for getting information about cities and towns in the United States.

Worldtime (http://www.worldtime.com/) is a service featuring an interactive world atlas. This reference tool also lists sunrise and sunset times for hundreds of cities. Worldwide public holidays are listed here, too.

PDS Mars Explorer for the Armchair Astronaut (http://www.pdsimage.wr.usgs.gov/PDS/public/mapmaker/) is really out of this world! OK, science buffs! How would you like to get an image map of any area on Mars? Choose a variety of zoom levels, image sizes, and map projections. These images were created using data from NASA's Viking space missions.

Complete Research Searching

Funk and Wagnall's Knowledge Center (http://www.fwkc.com) contains an amazing collection of knowledge from Funk and Wagnall's encyclopedia, the Random House Webster's College Dictionary, and Reuters World News. Another useful feature is the Media Index. This research tool provides you with photos, animations, maps, flags, and audio clips. Use the Power Search tool in order to probe all these resources for your keywords.

My Virtual Reference Desk (http://www.refdesk.com) must be home to the biggest desk in the world! What *doesn't* this site have? You could get lost clicking on all the fascinating tools here. Like clocks? You can see the USNO (United States Naval Observatory) atomic clock, plus a United States and world population clock. There's a homework help section and "ask the experts." There's a ton of search engines as well as a 50-volume encyclopedia. And don't forget current news! This part of the desk features hundreds of publications, live television and radio feeds, business news, weather, and sports. And if you need a break, check out comics, crosswords, Fun Stuff, and Free Stuff. If you really just want to get to work, use the MVRD search. It lets you search this site (and all its tools) or the World Wide Web. Instead of providing articles, this encyclopedia and search engine return lists (long lists) of links related to your topic. Some topics are very well covered but you might occasionally run into a dead end.

The Whole Research Enchilada

Some research sites are like reference book sets. They don't have just a dictionary or an encyclopedia. You can look for information in several research resources. Sites like this may include a dictionary, an encyclopedia, a thesaurus, a news index, an atlas, and so on. Usually, you can use each tool separately or use a "power search" option to quickly look through the entire site for information.

This sort of research tool doesn't exist outside of the Web. You would need to find—and carry—each of the volumes. Think of lugging around just a dictionary and an encyclopedia! That alone would be quite a chore. Plus, online research sites usually have many more tools. One search looks for your topic in several reference sources. And these sites usually have links in their articles, too, to help you find even more information.

Still Looking?

Do you want to unearth some cool sites of your own? Where should you start? Good question. Remember the chapter on searching, earlier in the book? (See pages 46–61.) Here's a great way to use those tips. You could use a traditional search engine. Type in "encyclopedia" and start clicking around those hits. It is a good idea to use directory searches here. Many search engines have reference categories built right in!

Search Engine Reference Resources

Check out the search engine references below when doing research. But remember: Practice makes perfect! If you don't find what you are looking for right away, keep looking.

Yahooligans! School Bell: Reference
(http://www.yahooligans.com/School_Bell/Reference)

Excite Reference (http://www.excite.com/reference)

Infoseek: Education: Reference
(http://www.infoseek.com/ Topic/Education/Reference)

AltaVista: Reference & Education
(http://jump.altavista. com/cat/refr)

Lycos: Education: Reference
(http://www.lycos.com/ wguide/network/net_484451.html)

HotBot: Reference (http://www.hotbot.com/reference)

Chapter 8
School Subjects

Your day at school isn't spent doing just one thing. Your class might work on math problems first thing in the morning. Then your teacher might give a lesson in social studies. You might have an art class just before lunch. In the afternoon, your class might work on science experiments. Before you go home, you might spend time reading aloud in groups.

Schoolwork involves a lot of different subjects. In elementary and middle school, these subjects are usually language arts, social studies, science, math, and the arts. And just like the megadirectories on the Web, each of these subjects includes many different topics.

Language Arts

Language arts is the study of language. It includes both reading and writing. Alphabets, spelling, phonics, grammar, and vocabulary are some of the building blocks of language arts. But language arts doesn't only involve studying English. Foreign language is also a language art. If you study a foreign language, you will study its vocabulary, spelling, and grammar. You will also learn how to read, write, and speak it.

The Web can be a fun and useful addition to your schoolwork in language arts. Working on your skills on your own will really help you when it comes time to do work at school.

Some language arts Web sites offer games and quizzes to help you with spelling, grammar, or vocabulary. Others recommend great books for you to read. Still others help you with writing. The Web can help you brainstorm for a topic, find information, and get writing. And don't think that writing is something that should only be done for school. Do some creative writing on your own time. You may find that writing your own stories is a lot more exciting than watching a TV show. Both reading and writing go hand in hand. The more you read, the better you will be able to write (and vice versa). These two skills will stay with you throughout your life and they will always come in handy. Get some ideas on how to start working on your language arts skills at these Web sites:

Biography Maker (http://www.bham.wednet.edu/bio/bio-maker.htm) wants "to inspire lively story telling and vivid writing which will make your readers want to know more about your subject." This site walks you through all of the important steps of writing a biography, which include questioning, learning, and storytelling. Make sure you take a look at the "Six Traits of Effective Writing." Stop by this site in the early stages of preparing a biography. It will help you develop the skills necessary to becoming a better writer, which not only helps you in English class but will also help you in other subjects.

OH! Kids Language Arts: Writing (http://www.oplin.lib.oh. us/ oh_kids) wants to help you learn more about language. This site is published by the Ohio Public Library Information Network. The Subject Index covers such important topics as grammar, spelling, and writing. Make sure you take a look at the options available under the "Especially for Young Writers" heading in the Writing section. Improve your writing skills and take time to read what other kids have been writing.

Children's Literature Web Guide (http://www.ucalgary.ca/ ~dkbrown/) lists all sorts of resources for eager readers. It guides you to award-winning children's books, reading-related Web sites, book discussions, and lots of other resources. Remember to try to read as much as you can—good readers are better learners. Browse around this site to find a good book. Then head to the library and pick it up!

Grammar Gorillas (http://www.funbrain.com/grammar/index.html) will test your grammar skills. This page is part of the great Funbrain site. You can play a beginner or advanced game of Grammar Gorillas. You play by choosing the correct part of speech requested. Win bananas for each right answer! If you really go ape and get all of the questions correct, you can add your name to the list of other grammar aces.

Vocabulary Puzzles (http://www.vocabulary.com). You probably know all about vocabulary tests. This site, the home of Vocabulary University, takes a new spin on learning words by having you figure out fun puzzles. Each section of the test features questions that involve similar types of words. New games are posted every so often and the folks who run this cool online school are always adding new features to the site. Learning new words will help you with your reading, writing, and speaking—and that sure covers a lot! Enroll today and start working your way toward graduating from Vocabulary University!

Social Studies

Social studies is really several subjects in one. Social studies combines the study of history, different cultures, government, current events, and geography.

In social studies, you can learn all about what happened in the past: explorers, discoveries, inventions, times of war, and times of peace. You can learn about how the United States government works. Look into the past to see how our government was formed or study an upcoming presidential (or local) election. You'll also learn about other cultures and their governments. Today's current events become tomorrow's history and they're all a part of social studies. It can be really interesting to see how our world has developed.

The Web is a great resource for learning more about what is happening every day to change our world. The more you learn about what goes on all around you, the better informed you will be in school when it comes time for social studies.

Geography relates directly to everybody in the world. We all have our own place on the map, whether we live in: Portland, Maine; Portland, Oregon; or Portland, Victoria, in Australia! Studying maps helps you understand our world and the people who live in it. There are all kinds of maps on the Web— zoom-in on a map of your local area or another country.

Visit the Web and see how it can help you in your social studies: take a virtual tour of the White House; read Congressional bills and Supreme Court decisions; visit a wire service and read up-to-the-minute news; drop by the United Nations and read about human rights and economic development all over the world; learn about famous people; or visit historical museums to get a picture of the past. Learn about your country or see the world at these social studies sites:

Biography Online (http://www.biography.com) is a great resource for kids who are looking to learn the important facts about somebody famous from the past or present. This site features over 20,000 profiles kids can search for and browse through. Stop here when you are doing research for a report or just to learn more about the people who shape our world (and gain an edge in social studies). Learning about the past helps us understand the present a little better.

IPL Culture Quest (http://www.ipl.org/youth/cquest) is a great resource for inquisitive kids to visit. This page, posted by the Internet Public Library, celebrates societies around the world. Visit any part of the earth through this site. Culture Quest has broken the world down into eight convenient regions. Get better acquainted with different parts of the world, as well as the art, customs, and history of the people who live there. You just might find an interesting topic to write about for an upcoming school report.

The Smithsonian (http://www.si.edu) Web site, like the collection of museums in Washington D.C., is a national treasure. The Smithsonian site features museums, art galleries, and much, much more. Check out the Site Index to get an idea of how much this site has to offer. For instance, in the Native American History and Culture section, kids can check out all kinds of information on Native Americans. Being well-informed about topics that interest you will open more doors to learning and experience than you can imagine.

Science

Science can help you explore all kinds of things about our planet Earth—and other worlds, too! Science covers a lot of ground: life, energy, motion, heat, force, space, elements, matter, and more! Science studies everything that makes everything exist and happen the way that it does. Sounds pretty wild, huh? Well, it is!

Science lets you travel to the moon or to another universe. It lets you look into a living human body to see how life works. Learn why some people have blue or brown eyes and why others have one of each! It shows you the power of the earth's wind, water, and weather and the sun's awesome power, too. Science can even explain everyday things, such as why you lean forward if the car you're riding in suddenly slows down (it's called "inertia" and it's a powerful force). Did you know that color is actually created by light? Or that gravity holds us all onto earth and makes us weigh what we do? On the moon, where gravity is much less of a force, you would be much lighter! And don't forget the power of time—it turns coal into diamonds and moves the continents around like bath toys. Science explains everything—or at least it tries to.

The Web can be an important aid in your science schoolwork. Just like other school subjects, there is so much that you could study, there just isn't enough time in the day to cover everything! Exploring more of what you study in school on your own time will give you the chance to come across subjects that are really out of this world. And then, as you continue to study more in school, you will have plenty of ideas stored-up about all sorts of subjects! Visit these super scientific Web sites to see where they can lead you:

Discovery Channel Online (http://www.discovery.com) is your ticket to parts of the earth you have probably never seen. Feature Stories is a great place to begin exploring. Read all about scientific discoveries around the world. Topics here cover a lot of ground: natural science (such as volcanoes and earthquakes); space sciences; weird science (such as cosmic dust and sonic booms); plants and the environment; and much more. Dig into some new scientific topics and get a jump on your studies in school. You could easily spend a lot of time browsing around this site. Or just use the Search function to find exactly what you are looking for.

The Electronic Zoo (http://netvet.wustl.edu/e-zoo.htm). This site is really wild. Animals are the focus here: animal facts, animal care, veterinary science, and links and resources galore. The What's New section will keep you up-to-date on any veterinary science news. And if you want to learn all about a specific type of animal, check out Animal Resources. This section has one of the best collections of animal science links available on the Web. Stop here when you're doing a report on animals or if you just want to learn more about the animals you see living in your neighborhood. When we learn more about how the different elements of our world live, it connects us to them mentally and physically.

Exploratorium (http://www.exploratorium.edu/) is the online home of the Exploratorium museum in San Francisco, California, where visitors get to dig into science experiments. This site puts some of the best science exhibits and experiments online for kids to look at and try. Visit some of the Exploratorium's great exhibits in the Digital Library. Spend some time in the Learning Studio trying some science activities. Working on science in your spare time will really give you an edge in school by giving you firsthand experience with scientific exploration—that's what being a real scientist is all about!

The Franklin Institute Science Museum (http://sln.fi.edu/) has loads of online exhibits that cover almost every branch of science. For example, the EARTHFORCE section digs into earth science and Undersea and Oversee is all about the ocean. The exhibits and articles are on cool, fun topics such as robots or the history of flight. Frankly, this site is one of the best on the Web. Spend some time here and brush up on history and science all at once. And come back often—this site is always adding something new for kids to get into.

Math

Math is the study of numbers. That may sound simple at first, but math studies *all about* numbers: how they work; how they are related to each other; how they are combined; how to measure them; how they change—well, you get the idea.

You started learning math as a small child. Your parents and picture books probably helped you learn to count. From there you learned about numbers and what they stand for. Then you learned to add and subtract, multiply and divide. And the process continued through school as you learned about fractions, decimals, and word problems. In the future you will dive into algebra, geometry, trigonometry, and maybe even calculus. All of these math subjects build on one another like bricks in a house. And there is room for the World Wide Web in that house.

One way the Web can help you with math is through homework help. A lot of sites will answer questions that you have through e-mail—your own, personal online tutor! But there is much more to these sites than just questions and answers.

Some sites will help you brush-up on math skills while you play a game. Other sites pose mathematical puzzles, riddles, and exercises for you to solve. Another way to explore math on the Web is—get this—by reading stories! These mathematical tales will really tease your brain!

By working on math on your own, with the help of the Web, you will be training yourself to think faster and more clearly. Those skills will not only help you with your math at school, but in all of the other areas of your life. Get cracking on your math skills with the help of these Web sites:

Ask Dr. Math (http://forum.swarthmore.edu/dr.math) is the ultimate mathematics homework helper. If you are ever stuck on a problem and don't have anybody to turn to for help, don't freak out! Just call the doctor. Helpful folks who can field your math questions online are always only a few moments away. Answers to frequently asked questions (FAQs) are stored in the Archives—check there first for the solution to your problem. And if you can't find an answer, ask Dr. Math. Motivated math maniacs can find links to other sites that feature fun problems to try and solve. Always trying your hardest to figure out difficult problems will help train your mind to work better. There is no limit to how far you can go!

Mathmania (http://www.csr.uvic.ca/~mmania) always tries its best to challenge its visitors. A good place to start is in the Stories section, where you can read amusing mathematical tales that will also make you think. At this site you can also find problems to solve, activities to work on, exercises, tutorials, and more. Whether or not you are already into math, stop by Mathmania to see if you can solve some of the problems they pose. Constantly challenge yourself to try new things. Doing so will not only open up new ways of doing tasks at school, but you will find that math can help you understand more about the everyday world we live in.

Math Baseball (http://www.funbrain.com/math/index.html) lets you take a swing at solving math problems. When you show up at this online ballpark, you choose the style of math to be played. Work with one task, such as multiplication, or try several math skills at once. Then choose a skill level from Easy, Medium, Hard, or Super Brain. The pitcher will throw a problem at you, such as "6×5 =" and if you answer correctly, you'll get a single, double, triple, or home run depending on how hard the question was. Have fun and practice math at the same time. Just like playing a sport or a musical instrument, you need to practice school skills in order to stay sharp.

The Arts

A lot of your other school subjects are related to one another. In the same way, everything else that you learn can be applied to the arts. Visual arts (such as painting, drawing, scupture, and crafts) and musical arts (creating and listening to music) are a lot of fun to do and see. Appreciating and creating art is a skill that is developed through study and practice. And it is a great way to express yourself. By doing so, you will be developing a unique way of telling other people what you really think—and it will help make you smarter and a better student. For instance, did you know that over 80 percent of the people who worked on the Mars Pathfinder project studied music or art (or both) as children? (Pathfinder was a space mission to Mars.)

Art in elementary school is usually hands-on. You get to do all kinds of projects, such as finger-painting, clay sculpture, papier-mâché, mosaic tile, and more. There's more to art than getting your hands dirty, though.

For example, you can learn about different artists from the past, what types of art they created, and what their art meant to other people. This type of art is known as art history. Or you could study all about a certain type of art, such as how to paint people. Getting really good at any type of art is usually a long process, but it is a lot of fun to work on. And the Web can help you develop your interest in the arts.

Another side of art is music. Some studies show that studying music can actually make you smarter. And some research even shows that listening to classical music—especially music by Wolfgang Amadeus Mozart—can help your brain work better and make learning easier. This hasn't been proven yet, but it is interesting. Music is a lot of fun, and if it happens to make you smarter too, great! Some of the muscial things you can do online include taking piano lessons and listening to and learning about all kinds of music.

You can visit world famous museums on the Web as well. Take a look at—and even learn *how* to look at—some of the master- pieces decorating these online halls. Get some help develop- ing an appreciation for the arts, or get some ideas for making some art of your own with these creative sites:

Children's Music Web (http://childrensmusic.org) always has something to tempt your ears. Check out the currently fea- tured composer and learn about some muscial history. Or you can just listen to some seasonal songs. This site also features reviews of music, interviews with musicians, and related arti- cles. Take the Kids' Tour in order to learn new songs, post messages for other music lovers to read, find out about upcoming concerts and good radio stations in your area, and find lots of other musical news and information. Expand on the music knowledge you have learned in school and take some new information back to your classmates. Chances are, it will be music to their ears!

Musical Instrument Encyclopedia (http://lehigh.edu/zoellner/encyclopedia.html) is a great place to start learning about musical instruments. Here you can take a tour of various types of instruments. Each entry features the instrument's history, how it is formed, and how it is played. You can even hear some of the sounds the instrument makes by clicking "Play It" whenever it appears next to the entry. Find an instrument that looks interesting to you and then look into possibly playing it for the school band! Creating music is even more fun than listening to it, and you'll be developing a new skill that can last a lifetime.

The Piano Education Page (http://www.unm.edu/~loritaf/pnokids.html) is a super site for kids who already play the piano, those who are looking to start, and even for kids who just want to learn more about composers and the piano. You can also listen to selections of piano music at this site. They give suggestions on how to get more from your piano lessons and you can even ask a piano teacher for some advice. The folks at this site encourage you to listen to music as much as possible. Music is a great way to express yourself, both by playing and listening. And, by learning how to read and follow music, you will expand your language skills.

Metropolitan Museum of Art (http://www.metmuseum.org) is a nice way to introduce yourself to the world of art. Even if you can't visit the museum in person (and if you can, make sure you do), this site has a lot to offer. Browse the Collections section to see some art from around the world. Then pay a visit to The Education section. There are activities, games, and a lot of information that will help you learn more about art. As you learn more about the art that different people from around the world have created, you'll be learning more than just history. You'll be learning about societies from the past and present and how they have contributed to the world in which we all live.

It All Gets Caught in the Web!

Some Web sites offer a wealth of information on virtually any content area that you wish to explore. They have many topics, even more subtopics, and hundreds of links. These sites take you beyond the basics of language arts, social studies, science, math, and the arts. Visit the worlds of anthropology, nutrition, space biology, the theater, transportation, and more.

Homework Central (http://www.homeworkcentral.com/indexjr.html) has some great links. You could spend weeks at this site and never get through all of the information. You'll have to see it to believe it.

Study Web (http://www.studyweb.com) lists hundreds and hundreds of sites in over thirty categories. Each link is rated for grade level. That way you don't have to visit a site for math help only to find that it's only for high school or college kids!

Always Explore to Learn More

The sites in this chapter may seem like they can only offer you help with homework and school-related stuff. But they can do a lot more than that.

These sites dig deep into topics that you may have only heard a little bit about. Visiting them may not always help you find the answer to next week's science test, but they might help you find topics and subjects that interest you. They might even encourage you to explore further and learn more. And the more you learn in general, the better you will do in school. Not just because you have to, but because you want to! Follow links that look interesting to you and a world of information will unfold. Happy exploring!

Chapter 9
Get Off the Computer!

Life does not revolve around the World Wide Web. In fact, just a few years ago, few people had ever heard of it! They certainly hadn't used it. The cool sites that we've talked about didn't exist. There is a lot more to life than the Web. But guess what? The Web can help you find those other things! Then it's time to get up, turn off the computer, and get busy.

Explore Your World

It may be hard to imagine, but this world has nearly 6 billion people on it. Some live in neighborhoods a lot like yours. Others live far away—some without running water, electricity, stores, or computers. Many others live in places somewhere in between those two. On the Web, you can learn about other kids from all over the world.

If you can peel your eyes off of the computer screen and look out the window, you might see something interesting. Nature! Sky! Birds and squirrels! Fresh air! On the Web, you can learn all about the outdoors and get some cool ideas for how to spend your time outside.

Open the door to these sites and see if any look inviting:

101 Things You Can Do to Help Save Animals (http://www.zooregon.org/Survival/whatyou.html) is great for animal lovers. To save endangered species, we need to protect their environments. Learn about ways to help at this wild site. There are tips here for you to use at home, on vacation, and while shopping. There are even some business tips that you can share with your mom and dad.

Consumer Product Safety Commission (or CPSC) (http://www.cpsc.gov) helps keep families safe. The CPSC wants to try and help prevent unnecessary injuries. At the 4 Kids page, you'll find out how to protect yourself and your family. Learn how to look for unsafe products and what to do about them. The Brain Busters safety quiz is loaded with tips.

U.S. Environmental Protection Agency (http://www.epa.gov/kids) wants you to join the Explorers' Club! Here, kids learn about the environment. Learn about land, air, animals, and recycling. Games, stories, and puzzles teach you hundreds of ways to protect your environment. Check out the Game Room, Art Room, and Science Room for more fun activities.

World Surfari (http://www.supersurf.com) was founded by ten-year-old "cybernaut" Brian Giacoppo in 1996. He takes you to a different country each month. Learn about the country's people, society, and history. The World Surfari Message Board is waiting for kids around the world to talk to each other. They post messages about where they live, their schools, the games and sports they play, or anything else that they feel like talking about. Do you have something to say?

Rainforest Action Network/Kids' Corner (http://www.ran.org/ran/kids_action). The rainforests need your help! Every day, old-growth rainforest trees that are home to millions of animals are being cut down and used as building materials. While it is important to build homes for our families, that does not mean it is OK to destroy the homes of rainforest animals in the process. This site provides sample letters you can use to send to politicians and suggestions for other steps to take. Plus, you can learn all about the rainforests—and the people and animals who live there.

GreatKids Network (http://www.greatkids.com) tells the stories of the hundreds of thousands of positive, young role models in the world—some who we may run into in our communities! You're invited to tell your stories about a GreatKid in your family, school, or community. This site will eventually lead to a GreatKids television show!

Learn a New Skill

One great thing about the Web is that it can help you learn new skills or start a hobby. These skills may make your life more fun or they might be helpful. Some are both. Let's do some browsing and see what new skills we can pick up!

Rescue 411—First Aid Basics (http://library.advanced.org/ 10624/index.htm). Someday you might be faced with a life-or-death situation that requires quick action. You might be babysitting a child who burns herself with hot water. You may be the only one around when someone falls down and is knocked unconscious. Will you know what to do? Unfortunately, many times the answer is no. Learn important first aid basics at this site and play "You Bet Your Life!" This interactive game show lets you see how sharp you are at first aid.

Use a Compass (http://www.angelfire.com/fl/compless/ intro.html). Compasses use the earth's magnetic field to point out direction. They look like watches with N, E, S, and W instead of numbers. Take this compass lesson and learn how to use one. Then do some exploring!

Magic Tricks! (http://www.conjuror.com/magic-tricks) provides instructions for new magicians. This site teaches you tricks you can do with items from around your house. Make sure to get help from an adult when you want to try any potentially dangerous tricks. Once you've mastered those, you can move onto the material for advanced magicians.

Gardening for Kids (http://www.geocities.com/EnchantedForest/Glade/3313). Want to grow a beautiful garden of flowers? Check out this site! Start with basic tips—from soil to water to mulch. You'll get the foundation of gardening. Learn about different plants in the flower archives. Kid-friendly plants are easy to work with and dazzling!

Get Active and Healthy

American kids spend more time in front of the TV—and computer—than they do exercising. Exercise doesn't have to be a boring class—it can be lots of fun! Riding your bike, playing kickball, or just running around are all great ways to exercise. The Web can give you some ideas for fun exercise, too. Shake your bones after checking out these sites:

Benny Goodsport and the Goodsport Gang (http://www.bennygoodsport.com) teach that fitness is fun for everyone! Go on adventures like nature walks and fishing trips. Good Stuff To Do has puzzles and games. They are fun and teach about safety, fitness, and nutrition. You can enter contests, too.

Fitness Link's Fitness for Kids (http://fitnesslink.com/changes/kids.htm) features KidsLink. It's a question and answer column on health, just for kids. Get information on exercise for kids here, too. Check out Make Exercise a Habit and Fitness for Special Interests. You can find some great ways to exercise that you probably never thought of!

Crafts

Arts and crafts are great ways to express yourself. Plus, you can make nice things to decorate your room, give as gifts, or for school projects. Get creative after visiting these sites:

Joseph Wu's Origami Page (http://www.origami.vancouver. bc.ca) has a gallery of origami and diagrams on how to make a frog, crane, clothing, and more. Under Information, you can read about the history of paper folding.

Make Stuff (http://www.makestuff.com) is a fantastic site for making crafts. Click on Kid Stuff for great, kid-oriented projects. It includes fun and easy arts and crafts and cooking projects. They show you where to get good catalogs and free stuff, and they have a reading room to relax in after you've done a project. They also have an online search engine.

In the Kitchen

Who doesn't love to eat? Use these sites to learn to make some goodies of your own. Good food can be good for you. These sites provide recipes that you can make in your kitchen (ask a parent for help). And you might even learn a little about nutrition along the way. Get hungry and take a bite out of these sites:

Kids Food CyberClub (http://www.kids-food.org/kf_cyber.html) has a food guide, recipes, books about food, how to grow veggies and fruits, nutritional information, and activities. Use your online research skills to answer the question of the month. Learn about nutrition with the USDA's Food Guide Pyramid. You can even "Rate your Plate." The Club Cookbook has some delicious, nutritious, and easy recipes. Try Ants on a Log, Homemade Pizza, and Veggie Salad. Submit your favorite recipes too. Follow links to other cool kids' sites that feature on food, gardening, cooking, crafts, and writing.

Kids Kitchen (http://www.scoreone.com/kids_kitchen). Looking for recipes for really messy foods? Check out Kids Kitchen, where kids from around the world submit recipes for their messiest, yummiest creations. Try a Bird's Nest, Pasta Pie, Hedgehogs, and more! There are also sections with recipes for munchies and sweets. These are neater, but still delicious. Kids pick the best recipe each month. The site's bulletin board lets you swap recipes and make friends.

Learn a Language

If you haven't had the chance to learn a foreign language in school, you can give it a try on the Web. Or if you have had some instruction, check out these sites to brush up.

French (http://www.jump-gate.com/languages/french). This site teaches you to read and write French with several lessons. Start with grammar basics. Then, move to common phrases and sentences. Eventually (if you stick with it), you might be able to read the copies of Paris's *Le Monde* newspaper, which is available at the site.

Spanish (http://www.DocuWeb.ca/SiSpain/english/course/calgary/intro.html). This is a downloadable course from Canada's Spanish embassy. It has several lessons. Always ask your parents before downloading any files.

Chinese (http://www.indiana.edu/~chasso/auchinese.html). This is an audio lesson in Chinese. Listen to and learn hundreds of essential Chinese phrases. Learn how to say "how are you" and "good-bye." Move onto phrases and words you would need for dining and shopping in China.

Chef Stephen (http://www.kiva.net/~penguin/stephen.html). Stephen Craton tells you about his family and why he wants to be a chef. He also shares some favorite recipes with you. Try his Les Cochons dans la Couverture—that's Pigs in a Blanket in fancy French chef talk!

As you travel the Web, look for pages and sites that are interesting. You can use it to communicate, shop, learn, and study. Perhaps most important, you can use it to expand your horizons. It is hard to believe that a little box on your desk can take you anywhere on this planet—and let you look at other planets and solar systems. Some scientists have concluded that the invention of the Internet is as important as the invention of TV. Others say it is as important as the invention of the wheel! Either way, the Web is here to stay. Enjoy your time online, and be sure to make the Web a positive—and fun—influence in your life.

Glossary

Archive. An electronic attic for storing old information such as articles from an online magazine or questions answered by a homework expert. Web sites put out new information all the time, but they save all the old information in an archive.

Bookmark. A Web browser tool that makes it easy to find sites that you visit often. Also called Favorites in some browsers.

Browser. Software that reads and displays Web sites. Internet Explorer and Netscape Navigator are popular Web browsers.

CD-ROM. A disc that looks just like a music compact disc (CD) but stores computer programs.

Chat. An Internet feature that lets you type messages that appear on a friend's screen as soon as they type them. When several people get together to chat, they're in a "chat room."

Clip Art. Free-use pictures people download from the Web to use however they want. Clip art pictures used to be on paper, and people "clipped" them out of a book with scissors.

Copyright. A legal rule that says people own what they create. Nobody can download or use copyrighted pictures, sounds, or movies without permission from whomever created them. Make sure a Web site gives you permission to use its pictures before downloading them.

Download. Taking pictures, sounds, programs, or other information off the Internet and putting it on your computer.

E-mail. An Internet feature that lets you send typed messages to friends. It's like a regular letter, except the message is electronic and travels quickly over the Internet. You can attach files, such as pictures and sound clips, to e-mail messages.

FAQs. Frequently Asked Questions. FAQs answer the questions people usually have when they first visit a site. Check out FAQs to see what's going on when first arriving at a site.

Favorites. *See* Bookmark.

HTML. Hypertext Markup Language. The programming language used to create Web pages. A lot of programs exist now that use HTML and make creating Web pages easier.

Hyperlink. Words on a Web site that you click to visit another Web page. Hyperlinks ("links" for short) are usually underlined and a different color than other words on the page.

Icon. A picture you can click that represents something on your computer, such as a program (such as your Web browser), folder, or function (such as the trash bin).

Interactive. A Web site or computer program that lets you enter information or control what happens on the screen.

Internet. The network that connects computers around the world. When a computer is connected to the Internet (or Net for short), that computer's user can access information other Internet users have displayed for them to see and read. It's like exploring new places, except the information travels over telephone lines and through a computer.

Java. A programming language that runs little programs on Web pages. Some games you play at a Web page use Java.

Keywords. Words you use to search for information posted on Web sites. You use keywords when working in search engines.

Link. *See* Hyperlink.

Megadirectory. A Web site, like a search engine, that helps users find information. Megadirectories usually list information as topics. These topics lead to other subjects, and so on.

Modem. A device inside of the computer (or sometimes outside) that lets the computer connect to a telephone line and talk with other computers around the world. A computer using a modem is making a phone call just like people do, except its conversations bring up Web pages and transfer e-mail instead of spoken conversations.

Mouse. A handheld tool used to point to things on a computer screen. Point the arrow on the screen at something and click the button by pressing and releasing it. Most mouses have a right-hand button that provides more functions.

Multimedia. Any information on the computer screen except for plain words, including pictures, sounds, and movies.

Net. *See* Internet.

Password. A secret word people use to get into Web sites that only let in members. When you join some Web clubs, you'll create a password and use it every time you visit the Web site.

RealAudio. A special program you can add to your Web browser in order to listen to recorded sounds and music online. Try out songs on CDs you're thinking of buying or hear sound clips from your favorite movies. RealAudio can be downloaded for free, and it's easy to add to the browser.

RealPlayer. Just like RealAudio, except it also lets you watch movies online.

Screensaver. A picture that comes up on a computer screen if the user hasn't used the computer for a while. Screensavers got their name because old monitors could be damaged if one image stayed on the screen too long. Screensavers displayed pictures that "saved" the screen from damage. Now screensavers are just for fun.

Search Engine. A Web site, like a megadirectory, that helps users find information. These services look through all of the

Web sites that they keep track of to find what you are looking for. A search engine is like the card catalog at the library—it is the best place to start looking for information.

Shockwave. A special program you can add to your Web browser so you can view animations such as cartoons and play lots of games. When visiting a site with features that need Shockwave, a message will let you know. You can download Shockwave for free, and it's easy to add to the browser.

Surfing. The word for cruising around the Internet. When people get done working online, they'll say something like, "I've been surfing for two hours."

URL. Uniform Resource Locator. The fancy name for a Web page's address. The address "http://www.pbs.org" is a URL.

User. Computer user. The name for people when they are "using" computers.

Virtual. Internet versions of things found in real life. A virtual postcard isn't a real postcard that you drop in the mail; it's an electronic message and picture that you send over the Net.

Web Page. The name for a document on the Web. Web pages are created in HTML.

Web Site. The name for a collection of Web pages on one topic put up by one person or group.

Web TV. A way, with the help of a set-top box (like a cable TV box), of displaying the Web on a TV instead of a computer.

World Wide Web. A way of viewing the Internet. The World Wide Web (or Web for short) is the group of connected Web pages and sites, featuring animation, photographs, pictures, text, movies, sound, and more. Many Web pages and sites— from all over the world—are linked together (*see* Hyperlink) and can be visited with the touch of a button.

Index